The Romance of Missionary Heroism

True Stories of the Intrepid Bravery and Stirring Adventures of Missionaries with Primitive Peoples, Wild Animals and the Forces of Nature in All Parts of the World

Volume 1: Asia and Africa

WITH ILLUSTRATIONS

by
John C. Lambert, M.A., D.D.

Schmul Publishing Company
Nicholasville, Kentucky

PUBLISHED 1979 BY SCHMUL PUBLISHING CO.

Published by Schmul Publishing Co.
PO Box 776
Nicholasville, KY 40340

Printed in the United States of America

ISBN 10: 0-88019-103-1
ISBN 13: 978-0-88019-103-6

Visit us on the Internet at www.wesleyanbooks.com, or order direct from the publisher by calling 800-772-6657, or by writing to the above address.

PREFATORY NOTE

THE author desires with much gratitude to acknowledge his debt to the following ladies and gentlemen, who have most kindly assisted him in gathering the materials for this book by giving their consent to his use of their writings, by lending him books and photographs, or in other ways:—

Miss Constance F. Gordon Cumming; the Rev. George Robson, D.D., Editor of the "Missionary Record of the United Free Church of Scotland"; the Rev. James Paton, D.D.; Mr. Fred S. Arnot, founder of the Garenganze Mission; the Picpus Fathers of the Damien Institute, Eccleshall; the Rev. E. P. Cachemaille, M.A., and Captain E. Poulden, R.N., the Secretaries of the South American Missionary Society; the Rev. J. W. Jack, M.A.; the Rev. W. MacNaughtan, M.A., of the Presbyterian Mission in Liao-Yang; Miss M. G. Cowan, Hon. Librarian of the Missionary Library at Lady Stair's House, Edinburgh; Mr. John Cochrane, of the Publications Office of the United Free Church; Mrs. D. R. MacKenzie, of the Livingstonia Mission, Lake Nyasa; Mr. R. K. Westwater.

He would also express his obligations to the following missionary societies and firms of publishers, which have most courteously allowed him to make use of the books mentioned in their proper places at the end of each chapter, and in some cases of illustrations of which they hold the copyright:—

The South American Society; The Religious Tract Society; The Society for Promoting Christian Knowledge; Messrs.

PREFATORY NOTE

Macmillan & Co.; The Clarendon Press; Messrs. Oliphant, Anderson, & Ferrier; The Fleming H. Revell Co.; Messrs. Hodder & Stoughton; Mr. T. Fisher Unwin; Messrs. S. W. Partridge & Co.; Messrs. Morgan & Scott; Messrs. Marshall Bros.; Messrs. Seeley & Co., Ltd.; The United Society of Christian Endeavour.

INTRODUCTION

IN a "foreword" which he contributes to Dr. Jacob Chamberlain's attractive missionary book, *In the Tiger Jungle*, Dr. Francis E. Clark expresses the opinion that one need not patronize sensational and unhealthy fiction to find stirring adventure and thrilling narrative, and then goes on to say:—

"There is one source which furnishes stories of intense and dramatic interest, abounding in novel situations and spiced with abundant adventure; and this source is at the same time the purest and most invigorating fountain at which our youth can drink. To change the figure, this is a mine hitherto largely unworked; it contains rich nuggets of ore, which will well repay the prospector in this new field."

The field to which Dr. Clark refers is the history of modern Christian missions. His meaning is that the adventurous and stirring side of missionary experience needs to be brought out, and emphasis laid upon the fact that the romantic days of missions are by no means past.

There are stories which are now among the classics of missionary romance. Such are the expedition of Hans Egede to Greenland, the lonely journeys of David Brainerd among the Indian tribes of the North American forests, the voyage of John Williams from one coral island of the Pacific to another in the little ship which his own hands had built, the exploration of the Dark Continent by David Livingstone in the hope of emancipating the black man's soul.

But among missionary lives which are more recent or less known, there are many not less noble or less thrilling than those just referred to; and the chapters which follow are an attempt to make this plain.

INTRODUCTION

There is, of course, a deeper side to Christian missions—a side that is essential and invariable—while the elements of adventure and romance are accidental and occasional. If in these pages the spiritual aspects of foreign mission work are but slightly touched upon, it is not because they are either forgotten or ignored, but simply because it was not part of the writer's present plan to deal with them. It is his hope, nevertheless, that some of those into whose hands this book may come will be induced by what they read to make fuller acquaintance with the lives and aims of our missionary heroes, and so will catch something of that spirit which led them to face innumerable dangers, toils, and trials among heathen and often savage peoples, whether in the frozen North or the burning South, whether in the hidden depths of some vast continent or among the scattered "islands of the ocean seas."

In the recently published *Memoirs of Archbishop Temple* we find the future Primate of the Church of England, when a youth of twenty, writing to tell his mother how his imagination had been stirred by the sight of Bishop Selwyn of New Zealand starting for the Pacific with a band of young men who had devoted themselves to the propagation of the Gospel among a benighted and barbarous people. "It is not mere momentary enthusiasm with me," he writes; "my heart beats whenever I think of it. I think it one of the noblest things England has done for a long time; almost the only thing really worthy of herself."

It is the author's earnest desire that the narratives which follow may help to kindle in some minds an enthusiasm for missions like that which characterized Frederick Temple to the very end of his long and strenuous life; or, better still, that they may even suggest to some who are looking forward to the future with a high ambition, and wondering how to make the most of life, whether there is any career which offers so many opportunities of romantic experience and heroic achievement as that of a Christian missionary.

CONTENTS

ASIA

CHAPTER I

IN THE STEPPES AND DESERTS OF MONGOLIA

PAGE

James Gilmour—His bold plan—Mongolia—Across the plains —Boarding in a lama's tent—A Mongol menu—Scotch porridge—Learning to ride—Gilmour as pedlar and tramp—Wolves and bandits—The man in the iron cage—The wounded soldier and the living skeleton—Robinson Crusoe turned missionary 13

CHAPTER II

IN THE COUNTRY OF THE TELUGUS

Indian race-groups—The Dravidians—The land of the Telugus —Dr. Jacob Chamberlain—A primitive ambulance—"The Divine Guru"—Under the "Council-tree"—The village Swami—A Mohammedan mob—Fight with a serpent —The "serpent destroyer" and the village elders—Some tiger adventures—A flood on the Godavery 29

CHAPTER III

A JAPANESE ROMANCE

Romantic Japan—The *daimio* and the stable boy—Thirsting for truth—In a junk to Hakodate—A schooner and a stowaway —A discovery in Hong-Kong—Arrival in Boston—Mr. Hardy and "Joe"—At Amherst and Andover—The Mikado's embassy —Neesima's educational dreams—Return to Japan—The "Doshisha"—The wooden cross and the living monument 46

CONTENTS

CHAPTER IV

"FROM FAR FORMOSA"

PAGE

George Leslie Mackay—A lawless land—The Malay and the Chinaman—Dentistry and the Gospel—A cruel plot—The capture of Bang-kah—The barbarians of the plain—The Kap-tsu-lan fishermen—The mountain head-hunters—A Christmas night in the head-hunter's house 62

CHAPTER V

A HEROINE OF TIBET

Mysterious Lhasa—The lady who tried to lift the veil—In the Himalayas—On the Chino-Tibetan frontier—the caravan for Lhasa—Attacked by brigands—The kilted Goloks—Among perpetual snows—A Tibetan love story—Noga the traitor—The arrest—Return to China—In the Chumbi Valley 78

CHAPTER VI

"THE SAVIOUR OF LIAO-YANG"

A medical missionary's power—The Boxer madness—The avenging Russians—Looting of Hai-cheng—The "Free Healing Hall"—In front of Liao-yang—"A fine thing done by a white man all alone"—"The Saviour of Liao-yang"—Russo-Japanese war—Battle of Liao-yang—A mission hospital in the hour of battle—Mr. Bennet Burleigh's testimony—A robber's point of view—Adventure with bandits . 93

AFRICA

CHAPTER VII

"THE HERO OF UGANDA"

The kingdom of Mtesa—The young engineer—Victoria Nyanza —The *Daisy*—A *baraza* at Mtesa's court—The land of blood—"Makay lubare"—A Brobdingnagian coffin—King Mwanga and the martyrs—Murder of Bishop Hannington—A visit from Stanley—Mackay's death—An Easter Sunday in the Cathedral of Uganda 106

CONTENTS

CHAPTER VIII

THE LION-HEARTED BISHOP

PAGE

"Mad Jim"—An ideal pioneer—A novel way of landing in Africa—"Teek, teek, teek"—Encounter with lions—Turned back from the goal—Bishop of East Equatorial Africa— The new route to Uganda—Through Masailand—The El Moran—Greasy bed-fellows—The forbidden land—Martyrdom 121

CHAPTER IX

PIONEERS IN NYASALAND

Up the Zambesi and the Shire—Lake Nyasa—Dr. Livingstone and Livingstonia—The first pioneers—Gravestones and milestones—The wild Angoni—A raid and a rescue—A great *indaba*—Arab slavers—The Arab war—African Lakes Corporation—Transformation of Central Africa— A dream-city 140

CHAPTER X

VORTREKKERS IN BAROTSELAND

The three horsemen at the Great Kei River—Francois Coillard —Trekking northwards—In the clutches of Lobengula—In Khama's country—The Makari-kari Desert—The Upper Zambesi—King Lewanika of Barotseland—A canoe voyage —Adventure withthe Balubale—The coming of the Iron Horse 157

CHAPTER XI

A PIONEER IN GARENGANZE

King Msidi's letter—Garenganze—Fred S. Arnot—His earlier travels—The expedition from Benguela—An African camp —The beeswax hunters—Watershed of the continent—Reception by Msidi—A night with cheetahs and hyenas—Horrors of the slave traffic—The saviours of Africa 168

LIST OF ILLUSTRATIONS

THE ROMANCE OF MISSIONARY HEROISM

ASIA

CHAPTER I

IN THE STEPPES AND DESERTS OF MONGOLIA

James Gilmour—His bold plan—Mongolia—Across the plains—Boarding in a lama's tent—A Mongol menu—Scotch porridge—Learning to ride—Gilmour as pedlar and tramp—Wolves and bandits—The man in the iron cage—The wounded soldier and the living skeleton—Robinson Crusoe turned missionary.

ABOUT the middle of the year 1870 there arrived in Peking a young Scotchman, James Gilmour by name, who had been sent out to China by the London Missionary Society to begin work in the capital. Within a few weeks of his arrival, there took place at Tientsin, the port of Peking, that fanatical outbreak known as the Tientsin massacre, in which a Roman Catholic convent was destroyed and thirteen French people murdered. A widespread panic at once took hold of the capital. The European community felt that they were living on the edge of a volcano, for no one knew but that this massacre might be the prelude to a general outburst of anti-foreign hatred such as was witnessed later in connexion with the Boxer movement. All around Gilmour his acquaintances were packing up their most precious belongings, and holding themselves in readiness for a hurried flight to the south. It was at this moment that the new-comer resolved on a bold and original move. Instead of fleeing to the south in search of safety, he would turn his face northwards and see if no opening could be found for Christian work among the Mongols of the great Mongolian plains. He was utterly unacquainted both with the country and the language, but he had long felt a deep and romantic interest in that vast, lonely plateau which lies between China proper and Siberia, and forms by far the largest dependency of the Chinese Empire. The suspension of work in Peking seemed to offer the very opportunity he wanted for pushing his way into Mongolia. And so as soon as the necessary preparations could be made, for Gilmour was never the man to let the grass grow beneath his feet, he left the capital behind with all its rumours and alarms. Before long the Great Wall was passed, which ever since the third century B.C. has defended China from Mongolia. And then, with two camels and a camel-cart, our intrepid traveller set his face towards the Desert of Gobi, which lies in the very heart of the Mongolian plain.

Mongolia, the home of the Mongols, has been described as a rough parallelogram, 1800 miles from east to west, and 1000 miles from north to south. It is a huge plateau lifted high above the sea, in part desert, in part a treeless expanse of grassy steppe, and in part covered by mountain ranges whose peaks rise up to the line of perpetual snow. The climate, hot and dry in summer and bitterly cold in winter, makes agriculture impossible except in some favoured spots, and so by the force of his circumstances the Mongol is a nomad, dwelling in a tent, and pasturing his flocks and herds upon the grass of the steppe. For long centuries the people were a constant terror to the Chinese. Even the Great Wall proved an ineffectual barrier against them, and time and again they poured like a mighty flood over the rich lands of their peace-loving neighbours to the south. But about 500 years ago they were converted from their earlier Pagan faith to Buddhism in its corrupted form of Lamaism, and this change of faith has had a decidedly softening effect upon the national character. Much of this, no doubt, must be attributed to the custom which prevails among them of devoting one or more sons in every family to the priesthood. One result of this custom is, that the Mongol priests, or lamas as they are called, actually form the majority of the male population, and as the lamas are celibates in virtue of their office, another result has been a great reduction in the population, as compared with early days. It is calculated that at the present time there are not more than two millions of Mongols occupying this vast territory of 1,300,000 square miles. Mongolia is no longer entitled now to the name it once received of *officina gentium*, "the manufactory of nations." It does not now possess those surplus swarms of bold and warlike horsemen which it once sent out to overrun and conquer other lands. But, like all nomads, its people are still an active and hardy race. As horsemen, too, they still excel. From their very infancy both men and women are accustomed to the saddle, and even yet some of them could rival the feats of the horsemen of Ghengis Khan, the greatest of all the Mongol conquerors of long ago. It was to this country and this interesting, but little known, people that James Gilmour devoted his life.

His first journey across the great plateau began at Kalgan, which lies to the north-west of Peking, just within the Great Wall, and terminated at Kiachta on the southern frontier of Siberia. He made this journey over plain and desert, which occupied only a month, in the company of a Russian official who knew no English, while he himself knew neither Russian nor Mongolian. He was glad, therefore, on reaching Kiachta to meet a fellow-countryman, one of the world's ubiquitous Scots, in the person of a trader named Grant. Grant was exceedingly kind to him, and took him into his own comfortable house. But finding that this contact with civilization was hindering him in his strenuous efforts to master the Mongolian language without delay, Gilmour formed a characteristic resolution. This was nothing else than to go out upon the plain and try to persuade some Mongolian to receive him as an inmate of his tent.

It was at night that this idea occurred to him, and the next morning he left Kiachta, taking nothing with him but his "Penang lawyer." This, it should be explained, is a heavy walking-stick, so-called because in Penang it is supposed to be useful in settling disputes. Gilmour had already discovered that in Mongolia it was not only useful, but altogether indispensable, as a protection against the ferocious assaults of the wolfish-looking dogs which

IN A MONGOL ENCAMPMENT

Mr. Gilmour always dressed in Chinese clothes, and when on tour generally had a postman's bag strapped over one shoulder and a waterproof fishing-bag over the other, these two containing all his baggage.

invariably rush at a traveller if he draws near to any encampment. One of the first incidents of the caravan journey from Kalgan had been the narrow escape of a Russian soldier from being torn down by a pack of Mongolian dogs. With a stout "limb of the law" in his fist, however, Gilmour feared nothing, but strode cheerfully over the plain, making for the first tent he saw on the horizon.

As he drew near he heard the sound of a monotonous voice engaged in some kind of chant, and when he entered found a lama at his prayers. The lama, hearing footsteps, looked round and pronounced the one word, "Sit!" and then continued his devotions. For another quarter of an hour he went on, taking no further notice of his visitor meanwhile. But suddenly his droning chant ceased, and he came forward and gave Gilmour a hospitable welcome. Gilmour opened his mind to him without delay, telling him that it was his desire to spend the winter in his tent and learn Mongolian from his instruction. The lama was surprised, but perfectly willing, and agreed to receive his visitor as a paying guest for an indefinite period at the modest rate of about a shilling a day. And so within a few months of his departure from London we find Gilmour living the life of a nomad in the tent of a lama on the Mongolian plain.

Once the first novelty had worn off, he found the life somewhat monotonous. Dinner was the great event of the day, the more so as it is the only meal in which a Mongol indulges. The preparations for this repast were unvarying, as also was the subsequent menu. Towards sunset the lama's servant, who was himself a lama, melted a block of ice in a huge pot, over a fire which filled the tent with smoke. Taking a hatchet, he next hewed a solid lump of mutton from a frozen carcase and put it into the water. As soon as it was boiled, he fished it out with the fire-tongs and laid it on a board before his master and Gilmour, who then attacked it with fingers and knives. Forks were things unknown. When a Mongol eats he takes a piece of meat in his left hand, seizes it with his teeth, and then cuts off his mouthful close to his lips by a quick upward movement of his knife. The operation looks dangerous, but the flatness of the native nose makes it safe enough, though it would be very risky in the case of one who was otherwise endowed. The Mongols always thought Gilmour's nose tremendous, and they excused him for cutting off his mouthfuls first and appropriating them afterwards.

Meanwhile, as this first course was in progress, the servant had thrown some millet into the water used for boiling the meat, and when the diners had partaken sufficiently of the solid fare, this thin gruel was served up as a kind of soup. The mutton, Gilmour says, was tough; but he declares that seldom in his life did he taste any preparation of civilized cookery so delicious as this millet-soup. He admits that he has no doubt that it was chiefly desert-hunger that made it seem so good.

Though he ate only once a day, the lama, like all Mongols, consumed vast quantities of tea. At dawn, and again at noon, the servant prepared a pailful of the cheering beverage, giving it always ten or fifteen minutes' hard boiling, and seasoning it with fat and a little meal instead of milk. Gilmour accommodated himself to the ways of the tent. As a concession to his Scotch tastes, however, he was provided every morning with a cupful of meal made into something like porridge by the addition of boiling water. This the lama and his servant called "Scotland," and they were careful to set it aside regularly for the use of "Our Gilmour," to whom, Buddhist priests though they were, they soon became quite attached.

Before leaving the subject of meals, we may mention that on the last day of the year Mongols make up for their abstemiousness during the other 364 by taking no fewer than seven dinners. When New Year's Eve arrived, the lama insisted that his visitor should do his duty like a Mongolian, and a yellow-coated old lama, who was present as a guest on the occasion, was told off to keep count of his progress. Gilmour managed to put down three dinners, and was just wondering what to do next when he discovered that his guardian lama had got drunk and lost count. In this case, although himself a strict teetotaler, he did not feel disposed to take too severe a view of the old gentleman's failing.

When the time came at last to recross the plains, Gilmour decided to make the homeward journey on horseback instead of by camel-cart. The one drawback was that he had never yet learned to ride. But as he had found that the best way to learn Mongolian was by being compelled to speak it, he considered that a ride of a good many hundred miles might be the best way of learning to sit on a horse. The plan proved a decided success. In Mongolia a man who cannot ride is looked upon as a curiosity, and when Gilmour first mounted everybody turned out to enjoy the sight of his awkwardness. But though he had one or two nasty falls through his horse stumbling into holes on treacherous bits of ground, such as are very frequent on the plains, where the rats have excavated galleries underground, he soon learned to be quite at home on the back of his steed. When he rode at last once more through a gateway of the Great Wall, passing thus out of Mongolia into China again, he felt that after the training he had received on his way across the steppes and the desert, he would be ready henceforth to take to the saddle in any circumstances. Indeed, so sure of his seat had he become that we find him on a subsequent occasion, when he formed one of a company mounted for a journey on Chinese mules, which will not travel except in single file, riding with his face to the tail of his beast, so as to be better able to engage in conversation with the cavalier who came behind him.

This crossing and recrossing of the Mongolian plain, and especially the winter he had spent in the lama's tent, had already given Gilmour a knowledge of the Mongolian language, and a familiarity with the habits and thoughts of the Mongols themselves, such as hardly any other Western could pretend to. Peking, when he returned to it, had settled down to something like its normal quiet, but he felt that the ordinary routine of work in the city was not the work to which he was specially called. The desert air was in his blood now, and Mongolia was calling. Henceforth it was for the Mongols that he lived.

Year by year Gilmour fared forth into the Great Plain in prosecution of his chosen task. And although it was his custom to return to Peking for the winter, he still continued while there to devote himself to his Mongol flock. Between China and Mongolia a considerable trade is carried on, the Mongols bringing in hides, cheese, butter, and the other products of a pastoral territory, and carrying away in return vast quantities of cheap tea in the form of compressed bricks, these bricks being used in Gilmour's time not only for the preparation of the favourite beverage, but as a means of exchange in lieu of money. During the winter months large numbers of traders arrive in Peking from all parts of Mongolia, and many of them camp out in their tents in open spaces, just as they do when living on the plains. Gilmour frequented these encampments, and took every opportunity he could make or find of conversing about religious matters, and especially of seeking to commend "the Jesus-doctrine," as the Buddhists called it. One plan that he followed was to go about like a Chinese pedlar, with two bags of books in the Mongolian language hanging from his shoulders. All were invited to buy, and in many cases this literature was taken up quite eagerly. Often a would-be purchaser demanded to have a book read aloud to him before he made up his mind about it, and this gave the pedlar a welcome chance of reading from the Gospels to the crowd which gathered, and then of introducing a conversation, which sometimes passed into a discussion, about the merits of Jesus and Buddha. Sometimes those who were anxious to buy had no money, but were prepared to pay in kind. And so, not infrequently, Gilmour was to be seen at night making his way back to his lodgings in the city "with a miscellaneous collection of cheese, sour-curd, butter, millet-cake, and sheep's fat, representing the produce of part of the day's sales."

GILMOUR AS TRAMP

Among the most remarkable of Gilmour's many journeys through Mongolia was one which he made in 1884, and made entirely on foot. He was a tremendous walker at times, more perhaps by reason of his unusual will power than because of exceptional physical strength, and is known to have covered 300 miles in seven and a half days—an average of forty miles a day. On the occasion of his long tramp over the plains and back, he had special reasons for adopting that method of locomotion.

One was that grass was so scarce during that year that it would hardly have been possible to get pasture for a camel or a horse. Another was that the love of simplicity and unconventionality, which was so marked a feature of his character, grew stronger and stronger, and also the desire to get as near as possible to the poorest and humblest of the people. At a later period we find him adopting in its entirety "not only the native dress, but practically the native food, and so far as a Christian man could, native habits of life." An idea of the length to which he carried the rule of plain living may be gathered from the fact that for some time his rate of expenditure was only threepence a day. His biographer, Mr. Lovett, gives us a graphic picture of him taking his bowl of porridge, native fashion, in the street, sitting down upon a low stool beside the boiler of the itinerant vendor from whom he had just purchased it. And the plainness of his garb at times may be judged of when we mention that in one village on the borders of China he was turned out of the two respectable inns which the place could boast, on the ground that he was a foot-traveller without cart or animal, who must be content to betake himself to the tavern for tramps.

It was in keeping with his tastes, therefore, as well as from necessity, that he once tramped through Mongolia with all his belongings on his back. His equipment when he set out consisted of a postman's brown bag on one side, containing his kit and provisions; on the other an angler's waterproof bag with books, etc.; together with a Chinaman's sheepskin coat slung over his shoulder by means of a rough stick of the "Penang lawyer" type. In the course of this tramp, his formidable stick notwithstanding, he had sometimes to be rescued from the teeth of the dogs which flew, not unnaturally, at a character so suspicious-looking. But he met with much hospitality from the people, both lamas and laymen, wherever he went; and returned to Kalgan without any serious mishap. From two dangers of the country he altogether escaped. One was the risk of being attacked by wolves, which are a perfect terror to the Chinese traveller over the plains, though the inhabitants themselves make light of them, and never hesitate when they catch sight of one to become the attacking party. The result of this is that a wolf is said to distinguish from afar between a Mongol and a Chinaman, slinking off as hastily as possible if it sees a wayfarer approaching in long skin robes, but anticipating a good dinner at the sight of another in blue jacket and trousers. Gilmour himself was of opinion that Mongolian wolves are not so dangerous as Siberian ones. The reason he gives is that, unlike the Russians, the Mongols keep such poor sheep-folds that a wolf can help itself to a sheep whenever it likes, and so is seldom driven by hunger to attack a man. The other danger was from bandits. For there are parts of the Desert of Gobi, crossed as it is by the great trade routes between Siberia and China, which are quite as unpleasant to traverse as the ancient road between Jerusalem and Jericho. But Gilmour was probably never more secure against highway robbery than when he walked through Mongolia as a missionary tramp.

It is impossible to enter into the details of the strange and romantic experiences which befel this adventurous spirit in the course of his many wanderings. Now we find him spending the night in a lama's tent, most probably discussing sacred things with his host till far on towards morning over a glowing fire of *argol*, or dried cow's dung, the customary fuel of the plains. At another time he is careering across the desert on horseback as swiftly as his Mongol companions, for he was a man who never liked to be beaten. Now he is at a marriage feast, looking on with observant and humorous eyes at the rough but harmless merry-makings. Again, he is in a court of justice, where punishment is meted out on the spot upon the culprit's back, in the presence of a highly appreciative crowd. At one time, with a heart full of pity for a superstitious and deluded people, he is watching a Buddhist turning his praying-wheel with his own hand or hanging it up in front of his tent to be turned for him by the wind. At another, as he passes a criminal in an iron cage who is condemned to be starved to death, and is set day by day in front of an eating-house in a large trading settlement for the aggravation of his tortures, he is reflecting on the defects of a religion that can permit its followers to enjoy this public exhibition of a fellow-creature's dying pains. In his journeys he was constantly exposed to the bitter cold of a land where the thermometer falls in winter to thirty or forty degrees below zero, and all through the heat of summer huge lumps of ice remain unmelted in the wells. Often he had to endure long spells of hunger and thirst when on the march. Worst of all, he had to share the filth and vermin of a Mongol tent as well as its hospitality. But these things he looked upon as all "in the day's work"; and though he may sometimes chronicle them in his diary as facts, he never makes them matter of complaint.

Among the most interesting incidents which he records are some in connexion with his endeavours to bring relief to those whom he found in sickness and pain. Although not a doctor by profession, he had picked up some medical and surgical skill, and did not hesitate to use it on behalf of those for whom no better skill was available. In doing this he sometimes ran great risks, for with all their hospitality the Mongols are terribly suspicious, and ready to entertain the most extraordinary rumours about the designs of any stranger.

Once he persuaded a blind man to come with him to Peking, to have his eyes operated on for cataract in the hospital there. The operation was unsuccessful, and the story was spread over a large region that Gilmour enticed people to Peking in order to steal "the jewels of their eyes" that he might preserve them in a bottle and sell them for hundreds of taels. In consequence of this he lived for months under what almost amounted to sentence of death. Only by showing no consciousness of fear and by patiently living suspicion down, did he escape from being murdered.

Once he had undertaken to treat a soldier for a bullet wound received in an encounter with brigands, thinking that it was only a flesh wound he had to deal with. It turned out to be a difficult bone complication. Now Gilmour knew hardly anything of anatomy, and he had absolutely no books to consult. "What could I do," he says, "but pray?" And a strange thing happened. There tottered up to him through the crowd a live skeleton—a man whose bones literally stood out as distinctly as if he were a specimen in an anatomical museum, with only a yellow skin drawn loosely over them. The man came to beg for cough medicine, but Gilmour was soon busy fingering a particular part of his skeleton, with so strange a smile on his face that he heard a bystander remark, "That smile means something." "So it did," Gilmour adds. "It meant among other things that I knew what to do with the wounded soldier's damaged bone; and in a short time his wound was in a fair way of healing."

James Gilmour's *Among the Mongols* is a book to be read, not only for the romance of its subject-matter, but because of the author's remarkable gift of realistic statement—his power of making his readers see things in bodily presence just as his own eyes had seen them. In more ways than one he reminds us of Borrow, but especially in what Borrow himself described as "the art of telling a plain story." On the first appearance of *Among the Mongols* a very competent reviewer in the *Spectator* traced a striking resemblance in Gilmour to a still greater writer of English than the author of *Lavengro* and *The Bible in Spain.* "Robinson Crusoe," he said, "has turned missionary, lived years in Mongolia, and written a book about it. That is this book." It was high praise, but it contained no small degree of truth. And to the advantage of Gilmour's book as compared with Defoe's, it must be remembered that everything that the former tells us is literally true.

AUTHORITIES.—*Among the Mongols,* by the Rev. James Gilmour, M.A., and *James Gilmour of Mongolia,* by Richard Lovett, M.A. (Religious Tract Society); *The Far East,* by Archibald Little (The Clarendon Press).

CHAPTER II

IN THE COUNTRY OF THE TELUGUS

Indian race-groups—The Dravidians—The land of the Telugus—Dr. Jacob Chamberlain—A primitive ambulance—"The Divine Guru"—Under the "Council-tree—The village Swami—A Mohammedan mob—Fight with a serpent—The "serpent destroyer" and the village elders—Some tiger adventures—A flood on the Godavery.

APART from the Tibeto Burman tribes scattered along the skirts of the Himalayas, the peoples of India are commonly divided by ethnologists into three great race-groups — the aborigines (often called the Kolarians), the Dravidians, and the Aryans. The aborigines are now found chiefly in the jungles and mountains of the Central Provinces, into which they were driven at a very early period by the Dravidians, the first invaders of India. Mr. Kipling, who has done so much to make India more intelligible to the English, has not forgotten to give us pictures of the aboriginal peoples. Those who are familiar with his fascinating *Jungle Books* will remember the story of "The King's Ankus," and the weird figure of the little Gond hunter who shot the villager with his feathered arrow for the sake of the jewelled ankus, and afterwards was found by Mowgli and

Bagheera lying in the forest beaten to death with bamboo rods by a band of thieves who lusted after the same fatal prize. In "The Tomb of his Ancestors," again, we have a vivid sketch of the mountain Bhils, whose combination of superstition, courage, and loyalty reminds us of the Scottish Highlanders in the days of Prince Charlie. These aborigines of the hills were long neglected by the Church, but much is now being done on their behalf. Dr. Shepherd, for example, a Scotch medical missionary, has carried both the Gospel and the healing powers of modern science into the wild country of the Bhils of Rajputana, and can tell tales of his experiences among them as striking and thrilling as any that have come from the pen of Rudyard Kipling.

The Dravidians, who first overran India and drove the earlier inhabitants into the hills, were afterwards themselves supplanted to a large extent by the more powerful Aryans. These Aryans were members of that same original stock to which the nations of Europe trace their origin, for while one section of the race moved southwards upon India through the Himalayas from the great plains of Central Asia, another flowed to the west and took possession of Europe. By the Aryan invasion of India the Dravidians were pushed for the most part into the southern portion of the vast peninsula, where they have formed ever since a numerous and powerful group. Five Dravidian peoples are usually distinguished, the Tamils and the Telugus being the most important of the five. It is of work among the Telugus that we are to speak in the present chapter.

The country of the Telugus stretches northwards from

Madras for some five hundred miles along the shores of the Bay of Bengal, while to the west it extends about half-way across the peninsula, and so includes large parts not only of the Presidency of Madras, but of the kingdom of Mysore and the dominions of the Nizam of Hyderabad. It is a region which attracts those who go to India for sport and adventure, for its jungles still abound in tigers and other wild animals. From the point of view of Christian missions it has this special interest, that there is no part of all Hindustan where the Gospel has been preached with more marked success, or where the people have been gathered more rapidly into the Christian Church. One of the most enterprising of modern Indian missionaries is Dr. Jacob Chamberlain, of the American Reformed Church, who began his labours as a medical evangelist to the Telugus more than forty years ago. He is the author of two books, *The Cobra's Den* and *In the Tiger Jungle*, which give graphic sketches of his experiences in city and village and jungle, on horseback and in bullock-cart, in the surgery with operating knife in hand, and at the busy fair when a crowd has gathered round and the knife that cures the body has been exchanged for the Book that saves the soul. Taking these two delightful volumes as our authorities, we shall first glance at Dr. Chamberlain in the midst of his medical and surgical work, and see how effective such work becomes in opening the way for Christian teaching. Then we shall follow him on one of his longer evangelistic tours through the Telugu country.

All morning, ever since sunrise, the doctor has been busy with the patients who have come from far and near to be treated or prescribed for, until about a hundred persons are gathered in front of the little dispensary. The heat of the day is now coming on, but before dismissing them and distributing the medicines they have waited for, he takes down his Telugu Bible, reads and explains a chapter, and then kneels to ask a blessing upon all who have need of healing.

It is now breakfast time, and after several hours of hard work the doctor is quite ready for a good meal. But just as he is about to go home for the purpose, he hears the familiar chant used by the natives when carrying a heavy burden, and looking out sees four men approaching, two in front and two behind, with a long bamboo pole on their shoulders, and a blanket slung on it in hammock fashion with a sick man inside. Behind this primitive ambulance two men are walking, one leading the other by the hand.

In a few minutes the sick man is laid in his blanket on the floor of the verandah, and the little company have told their tale. They have come from a village two days' journey off. They have heard of the foreign doctor that he can work wonderful cures. The young man in the blanket is dying; the old man led by the hand is his uncle, who has recently grown blind. Their friends have brought them to the Doctor Padre to see if he can make them well.

On examination Dr. Chamberlain finds that the young man's case is almost hopeless, but that there is just a chance of saving him by a serious surgical operation—and this he performs the same afternoon. At first the patient seems to be sinking under the shock, but he rallies by and by, and gradually comes back to health and strength again. The old man's blindness is a simpler case. An easy operation and careful treatment are all that are required. And so when uncle and nephew have been in the hospital for a few weeks, the doctor is able to send them back to their village—the young man walking on his own feet, and the old man no longer needing to be led by the hand.

But here the story does not end. Every day while in hospital the two patients had heard the doctor read a chapter from the Gospel and make its meaning plain. And when the time for leaving came they begged for a copy of the history of Yesu Kristu, "the Divine Guru," so that they might let all their neighbours know of the glad news they had heard. They acknowledged that they could not read, for they were poor weavers who had never been to school. "But when the cloth merchant comes to buy our webs," they said, "we will gather the villagers, and put the book into his hand, and say, 'Read us this book, and then we will talk business.' And when the tax-gatherer comes we will say, 'Read us this book, and then we will settle our taxes.' Let us have the book therefore, for we want all our village to know about the Divine Guru, Yesu Kristu."

They got the book and went away, and for three years Dr. Chamberlain heard nothing of them. But at last on a wide preaching tour he met them again. They had learned of his approach, and when he entered the village at sunrise the whole population was gathered under the "Council-tree," while his two patients of three years ago came forward with smiling faces to greet him, and told him that through the reading of the Gospel every one in the place had agreed to give up his idols if the Doctor

Padre would send some one to teach them more about Jesus. Dr. Chamberlain discussed the matter fully with them, and when he saw that they were thoroughly in earnest, promised to send a teacher as soon as possible. But just before leaving to proceed on his journey he noticed, near at hand, the little village temple, with its stone idols standing on their platform at the farther end of the shrine.

"What are you going to do with these idols now?" he said to the people.

"The idols are nothing to us any longer," they replied; "we have renounced them all."

"But are you going to leave them standing there in the very heart of the village?"

"What would you have us do with them?" they asked.

"Well," said the doctor, wishing to test their sincerity, "I would like to take one of them away with me." He knew the superstitious dread which even converted natives are apt to entertain for the idols of their fathers, and the unwillingness they usually have to lay violent hands on them. He did not expect anything more than that they might permit him to remove one of the images for himself. But at this point Ramudu, the old man whose sight had been restored, stepped forward and said, "I'll bring out the chief Swami for you"; and going into the shrine he shook the biggest idol from the plaster with which it was fastened to the stone platform, and then handed it to the doctor, saying as he did so something like this:—

"Well, old fellow, be off with you! We and our ancestor for a thousand years have feared and worshipped you. Now we have found a better God, and are done with you.

Be off with you, and a good riddance to us. Jesus is now our God and Saviour."

And so the ugly stone Swami that had lorded it so long over the consciences of these Telugu villagers was "dethroned," as Dr. Chamberlain puts it, "by the surgeon's knife," and passed in due course to a missionary museum in the United States. But Yesu Kristu, the Divine Guru, reigned in its stead.

But now let us follow the doctor in some of the more striking episodes of one of his earliest tours. It was a journey of 1200 miles, through the native kingdom of Hyderabad and on into Central India—a region where at that time no missionary had ever worked before. He rode all the way on a sturdy native pony, but was accompanied by four Indian assistants, with two bullock-carts full of Gospels and other Christian literature which he hoped to sell to the people at low prices.

One of their first and most dangerous adventures was in a walled city of Hyderabad. They had already disposed of a few Gospels and tracts when some Brahman priests and Mohammedan fanatics raised the mob against them It was done in this way. A number of the Gospels were bound in cloth boards of a buff colour. The Mohammedan zealots spread a rumour that these books were bound in pig-skin—a thing which no true disciple of Mahomet will touch. The Brahmans, on the other hand, told their followers that these yellow boards were made of calf-skin—and to a Hindu the cow is a sacred animal. The crowd got thoroughly excited, and soon Dr. Chamberlain and his four helpers were standing in the market-place with their backs to a wall, while a howling multitude surged in front, many of whom had already begun to tear up the cobblestones with which the street was paved in order to stone the intruders to death. The doctor saved the situation by getting permission to tell a wonderful story. Nothing catches an Indian crowd like the promise of a story. Their curiosity was aroused from the first, and soon their hearts were touched as they listened to a simple and graphic description of the death of Jesus on the cross. The stones dropped from the hands that clutched them, tears stood in many eyes, and when the speaker had finished every copy of the Gospels which had been brought into the city from the little camp without the walls was eagerly bought up by priests as well as people.

But dangers of this sort were rare. For the most part, both in town and country, the white traveller was welcomed courteously, and gladly listened to as he stood in the busy market-place or sat beside the village elders on the stone seat beneath the "Council-tree," and explained the purpose of his coming. Dangers of another kind, however, were common enough, and Dr. Chamberlain tells of some narrow escapes from serpents, tigers, and the other perils of the Indian jungle.

They were passing through the great teak forest, where the trees towered one hundred and fifty feet above their heads, when they came in sight one day of a large village in a forest clearing. As they drew near, the elders of the place came out to salute them. The doctor asked if they could give him a suitable place to pitch his tent, but they did better than that, for they gave him the free use of a newly erected shed.

Somewhat tired out with a long forenoon's march, Dr.

Chamberlain lay down to rest his limbs, and took up his Greek Testament meanwhile to read a chapter, holding the book over his face as he lay stretched out on his back. By and by he let his arm fall, and suddenly became aware that a huge serpent was coiled on one of the bamboo rafters just above him, and that it had gradually been letting itself down until some four feet of its body were hanging directly over his head, while its tongue was already forked out—a sure sign that it was just about to strike. He says that when studying the anatomy of the human frame he had sometimes wondered whether a person lying on his back could jump sideways, without first erecting himself, and that he discovered on this occasion that, with a proper incentive, the thing could be done.

Bounding from his dangerous position, he ran to the door of the shed and took from the bullock-cart which was standing there a huge iron spit five or six feet long, which was made for roasting meat in a jungle camp. With this as a spear he attacked the serpent, and was successful at his first thrust in pinning it to the rafter round which it was coiled. Holding the spit firmly in its place to prevent the struggling animal from shaking it out, though he ran the utmost risk of being struck as it shot out its fanged mouth in its efforts to reach his hand, he called loudly to his servant to bring him a bamboo cane. The cane was quickly brought, and then, still holding the spit in position with one hand, he beat the brute about the head till life was extinct. When quite sure that it was dead, he drew the spit out of the rafter and held it at arm's length on a level with his shoulder, the transfixed reptile hanging from it. He found that both the head

Dr. Chamberlain was quite unaware that a Huge Serpent was hanging over him and the tail touched the ground, thus showing that the serpent was not less than ten feet long.

Just at that moment the village watchman looked in at the door, and then passed on quickly into the village. And immediately it flashed into the doctor's mind that he had got himself into trouble, for he knew that these people worship serpents as gods. They never dare to kill one, and if they see a stranger trying to do so, will intercede for its life.

He was still considering what to do when he saw the chief men of the village advancing, and noticed, to his surprise, that they were carrying brass trays in their hands covered with sweetmeats, cocoanuts, and limes. His surprise was greater still when, as they reached the doorway in which he stood to meet them, they bowed down before him to the ground and presented their simple offerings, hailing him at the same time as the deliverer of their village. That deadly serpent, they told him, had been the terror of the place for several years. It had killed a child and several of their cattle, but they had never ventured to attack it, for they knew that if any of them did so he would be accursed. The kindred of the dead serpent would wage war upon that man and his family, until every one of them was exterminated. But their visitor had killed it without their knowledge or consent, and so they were freed from the pest of their lives, and at the same time were absolutely guiltless of its blood. Their gratitude knew no bounds. They pressed upon the doctor the fattest sheep in their flocks. They sent the village crier with his tom-tom all round the place to summon the people to come and hear the words of "the serpent-destroyer." And when Dr. Chamberlain seized the opportunity to speak to them about "that old serpent called the devil," and One who came to bruise the serpent's head, they listened to him as he had rarely been listened to before.

While serpents were, and still are, the most frequent danger of the traveller in the jungle, tigers were very numerous in the Telugu country forty years ago. Dr. Chamberlain has stories to tell both of the striped tiger, the royal tiger as it is commonly called, and the smaller spotted variety, which is marked like a leopard, but has a tiger's claws and cannot climb trees as a leopard can. On one occasion, when all alone and unarmed, he met a spotted tiger face to face on a narrow mountain path, but succeeded in putting the beast to flight by suddenly opening his big white umbrella and letting out a Red Indian war-whoop which he had learned when a boy from a tribe of American Indians in Michigan. An experience with a tiger of the larger sort, however, though less dramatic, was probably a good deal more dangerous.

It was about three weeks after their narrow escape from stoning in that walled city of Hyderabad, and they were still in the territories of the Nizam, but about one hundred miles farther north and in the midst of hill and jungle. The native assistants with the servants and bullock-carts had made an earlier start, and the doctor was riding on to overtake them when he noticed in the path, and side by side with the fresh cart tracks, the footprints of a huge tiger and its cub. He had been warned before plunging into the forest that seven people had recently been killed in this very neighbourhood by man-eating

ATTACKED BY A TIGER, WITH NO WEAPON BUT AN UMBRELLA

Dr. Chamberlain came face to face with a spotted tiger in a lonely mountain path, he had no weapon, but emitting a Red Indian war-whoop and suddenly putting up his umbrella, he put the animal to flight.

tigers; and it seemed evident that this tiger was following the carts with murderous intent. It is not the way of a tiger to attack a group of travellers. It watches and waits until one of them falls behind or gets detached from the rest, and then it makes its spring. Dr. Chamberlain realized the situation at once. The little caravan was safe so long as all kept close together, but if any one lagged behind the others, or stopped to quench his thirst at the wayside stream, the tiger would be on him in a moment.

Pulling out a loaded fourteen-inch Navy revolver, the only weapon he carried with him in his expeditions through the jungle, and dashing his spurs into his pony, he galloped on through the forest to warn those ahead. As he flew onwards his eye was on the path, and always he saw the cart tracks and the footprints of the tiger side by side. A deadly fear took hold of him that he might be too late. But suddenly there came a turn in the road, and there, not far in front, were the two carts and their attendants moving slowly and peacefully forward. And now the doctor noticed that the tiger tracks were gone. He had seen them last at the very corner round which the carts came into sight. Hearing the sharp tattoo of the pony's hoofs coming up behind, the tiger must have leaped into the bushes at that very point. Probably it was only a few feet from the horseman as he whisked past. But either his sudden appearance on his galloping steed gave it a fright, or else his motion was too rapid to offer the chance of a successful spring.

Not the least of the difficulties of travel in the wild parts of India is caused by the tropical floods. On one occasion Dr. Chamberlain and his little band were swept bodily down a river, usually fordable, but swollen now by recent rains. For a moment or two the doctor and his pony were submerged, but ultimately the whole company managed to swim or scramble safely to the opposite bank.

But it was a flood on the great Godavery river and its affluents that caused the worst predicament of all. By that time they had reached the extreme point of the expedition, up among the mountain Gonds, and had turned to the south-east to make the return journey by a different route. At a certain point they found that the steamer on which they had counted had broken down in attempting to stem the furious current, and that there was nothing for it but to march through seventy-five miles of a jungly, fever-haunted swamp in order to reach another steamer lower down. Bullock-carts were of no use, but by the aid of a *hookam* or firman from the Nizam himself which the doctor had got hold of, he succeeded in obtaining a large body of bearers from a native deputy-governor. These men, however, though promised threefold wages, were most unwilling to accompany him, for with the country in flood the jungle becomes a place of special dangers; and it was only by much flourishing of the afore-said Navy pistol, though without any intention of using it, that the doctor could make his men march at all or keep them from deserting.

But by and by an unforeseen trouble emerged. The constant dripping rain, the steamy heat, the jungle fever, the prowling tigers had all been taken into account. What had not been realized was the exceptional violence of the floods. And so one evening, when they came to a little tributary of the Godavery which must be crossed if they were to reach a place of safety for the night, they found that the backwater of the main stream, rushing up this channel, had made a passage absolutely impossible.

For a time they were almost at their wits' end, for it would have been almost as much as their lives were worth to spend the night in the midst of the swamp, and it was too late now to get back to the place from which they had started that morning. But guidance came in answer to prayer. Dr. Chamberlain tells us that all at once he seemed to hear a voice saying, "Turn to the left to the Godavery, and you will find rescue." And though the native guides assured him that to do so would only be a foolish waste of time and strength, as the Godavery was now a swirling flood three miles across, and no boat or raft could possibly be got within a distance of many miles, he made his men turn sharp to the left and march in the direction of the Godavery bank. To his great delight, and to the astonishment of the natives, the first thing they saw as they emerged from the bushes was a large flat boat, just at their feet, fastened to a tree on the shore.

The boatmen told them that early that morning their cables had snapped, and they had been carried away by the flood from a mooring station higher upstream and on the British side of the river. To this precise spot they had been swept, they could not tell how. But to Dr. Chamberlain and his four native evangelists it seemed clear that God had sent this boat expressly for their deliverance. They pitched their tent on the broad deck, and kindled a large fire on the shore to keep wild beasts away. And though the tigers scented them, and could be heard growling and snarling in the bushes that fringed the bank, the night was passed in comparative comfort and safety. Next day they floated down the stream towards the steamer that was to carry them southwards. And so ended the more adventurous part of this long missionary journey through the country of the Telugus.

Note.—The material for this chapter is derived from Dr. Chamberlain's two books already referred to, *The Cobra's Den* and *In the Tiger Jungle*, both published by Messrs. Oliphant, Anderson, and Ferrier.

CHAPTER III

A JAPANESE ROMANCE

Romantic Japan—The *daimio* and the stable-boy—Thirsting for truth—In a junk to Hakodate—A schooner and a stowaway—A discovery in Hong-Kong—Arrival in Boston—Mr. Hardy and "Joe"—At Amherst and Andover—The Mikado's embassy—Neesima's educational dreams—Return to Japan—The "Doshisha"—The wooden cross and the living monument.

THERE is no country on the map of the world with which it is more natural to associate the idea of romance than the island empire of Japan. The sudden awaking of the people from their sleep of centuries, their transition in the course of a single generation from something like European medievalism to the most up-to-date modernity, may fairly be described as one of the greatest wonders of history. Heroic as well as romantic, recalling twice over the immortal story of David and Goliath, are the two wars which the little Power has waged triumphantly in quick succession against the biggest empires—first of Asia and then of Europe. Romantic, too, as every traveller tells us, are the sights of the country and the ways of the people wherever Old Japan survives—the houses, the gardens, the elaborate courtesies, the artistic costumes, the combination of a frank naturalism with an artificiality which has become a second nature.

"DAIMIO" AND THE STABLE-BOY

In reading about Japan we sometimes feel as if we had to do not with the world of sober realities, but with a fascinating chapter out of a new volume of *Arabian Nights.* And yet even in a land in which wonders meet us on every side, the strange story of Joseph Neesima deserves to be called romantic.

He was born in 1843. It was ten years before that memorable Sabbath morning when Commodore Perry, of the U.S. Navy, with his fleet of "barbarian" ships steamed into the harbour of Uraga, in the Bay of Yedo, and extorted from a reluctant Government those treaties of friendship and commerce which broke down for ever the walls of seclusion behind which Japan had hid herself from the eyes of the world. Neesima was a *samurai*, a member of the old fighting caste of feudal times, and so even as a boy wore a sword and was sworn to a life of fealty to the *daimio* or prince on whose estate he was born.

From the first, however, it was evident that this little serf had a mind and will of his own, and also a passionate longing for truth and freedom. He devoted all his spare time to study, often sitting up over his books until the morning cocks began to crow. Once the prince, his master, caught him running away from his ordinary duties to go to the house of a teacher whom he was in the habit of visiting by stealth. After giving the boy a severe flogging, he asked him where he was going. Neesima's answer will best be given in his own words at a time when he had learned only enough English to write it in the "pidgin" fashion. "'Why you run out from here?' the *daimio* said. Then I answered him, 'That I wish to learn foreign knowledge, because foreigners have

Stereo Copyright Underwood & Underwood — London and New York

PRAYING TO IDOLS

A Japanese peasant girl saying her prayers to the stone images of Amida. The load on her back is firewood.

got best knowledge, and I hope to understand very quickly.' Then he said, 'With what reason will you like foreign knowledge? Perhaps it will mistake yourself.' I said to him sooner, 'Why will it mistake myself? I guess every one must take some knowledge. If a man has not any knowledge, I will worth him as a dog or a pig.' Then he laughed, and said to me, 'You are a stable-boy.'"

Not less remarkable than this thirst for knowledge was the lad's consciousness of the rights of human beings, and passionate desire for fuller liberty: "A day my comrade sent me a Atlas of United States, which was written in Chinese letter by some American minister. I read it many times, and I was wondered so much as my brain would melted out of my head, because I liked it very much—picking one President, building free schools, poorhouses, house of correction, and machine-working, and so forth, and I thought that a government of every country must be as President of United States. And I murmured myself that, O governor of Japan! why you keep down us, as a dog or a pig? We are people of Japan; if you govern us, you must love us as your children."

But above all young Neesima felt a deep longing after God. When he was about fifteen years of age, to the great distress of his relatives, he refused to worship any longer the family gods which stood on a shelf in the house. He saw for himself that they were "only whittled things," and that they never touched the food and drink which he offered to them. Not long after this he got possession of an abridged Bible history in the Chinese language, with which he was well acquainted, and was immensely struck by the opening sentence, "In the beginning God created the heaven and the earth." Immediately he recognized the Creator's claim to be worshipped. To this still Unknown God he began thereafter to pray, "Oh, if You have eyes, look upon me; if You have ears, listen for me."

Before long it became Neesima's constant desire to find his way to the port of Hakodate, as an open port, where he thought he might fall in with some Englishman or American from whom to obtain the knowledge that he wanted. He made application to the *daimio* to be allowed to undertake the voyage, but got only a scolding and a beating for his pains. Yet he did not despair. In the quaint language of his earliest English style, "My stableness did not destroy by their expostulations." He waited patiently for four or five years, and at last, to his inexpressible joy, secured permission to go to Hakodate in a sailing-junk which belonged to his master. The junk was a coaster, and it was several weeks before he reached the haven of his hopes. Getting to Hakodate at last, it seemed for a time as if nothing but disappointment was in store for him there. He could find no one to teach him English, and meanwhile his little stock of money melted rapidly away. At length matters began to look brighter. He fell in with a Russian priest who gave him some employment, and he made the acquaintance of a young Jap, Mr. Munokite, who was a clerk in an English store, and who not only taught him a little English, but helped to carry out a secret determination he had now formed of escaping to America at the earliest opportunity.

RESOLVES TO LEAVE JAPAN

He had not come to this decision without long and anxious thought. It involved great sacrifices and no small danger. In those days a Japanese subject was forbidden to leave the country on pain of death. If caught in the act of attempting to do so, he forfeited his life; while if he made good his escape, this meant that he had banished himself for ever from the "Land of the Rising Sun."

It was painful for the youth to think of leaving his parents without even saying good-bye, and with no prospect of ever seeing them again, especially as he had been brought up under the influence of the Confucian doctrine of filial obedience. But he thought the matter out, and saw at last that in the search for truth and God it may be proper to set all other claims aside. "I discovered for the first time," he wrote afterwards, "that the doctrines of Confucius on the filial relations are narrow and fallacious. I felt that I must take my own course. I must serve my Heavenly Father more than my earthly parents."

And Neesima loved his country as well as his home, for patriotism is a sentiment which glows with extraordinary warmth in every Japanese heart. Moreover, he was something of a poet as well as a patriot, seeing his country in the glowing hues of a lively imagination. The verses he wrote far out on the China Sea, after he had made good his flight, show how his heart kept turning back to the dear land of flowers. "If a man be determined in his mind to run away a thousand miles," one of his poems says, "he expects to have to endure great sufferings, and why can he be anxious about his home? But how strange! In the night, when the spring wind is blowing, in a dream he sees flowers in the garden at home."

But we are anticipating somewhat, for the story of Neesima's adventurous flight has yet to be told. After endless difficulties, his friend Munokite secured leave for him to work his passage to Shanghai on an American schooner, the *Berlin*, Captain Savory. He had, of course, to smuggle himself on board at his own risk, and to do so with the full knowledge that if detected by the harbour police he would be handed over to the executioner without delay. His plans had accordingly to be laid with the utmost caution. When night fell, he had a secret meeting in a private house with Munokite and two other young friends. They supped together, and passed round the *sake*-cup in token of love and faithfulness. At midnight the fugitive crept out of the house in the garb of a servant, carrying a bundle and following one of his friends who walked in front with a dignified air wearing two swords, as if he were the master. By back streets and dark lanes they found their way to the water's edge, where a small boat was already in waiting. Neesima was placed in the bottom of the boat and covered up with a tarpaulin as if he were a cargo of provisions; and then swiftly, but with muffled oars, the boatman pulled out to the schooner. A rope was thrown over the side, and the cargo, suddenly becoming very much alive, scrambled on board and hurried below.

That night he never slept a wink, for he knew that the worst danger was yet to come. In those days every vessel leaving Hakodate harbour was keenly searched at the last moment to make sure that no Japanese subject was secreted anywhere on board. Early next morning the police boat was seen coming off to the schooner for this purpose; and Neesima felt that his hour of destiny was at hand. But Captain Savory had laid his plans carefully too, for he also was running a risk; and he hid his dangerous passenger in a part of the ship where the watch-dogs of the port never thought of looking for him. The search was over at last; the anchor weighed; the sails spread to an off-shore breeze. The *Berlin* forged her way through the shipping and out to the open sea. Neesima now was safe and free. It was on 18 July, 1864, and the hero of our story was 21 years of age.

After a very disagreeable passage to Shanghai and ten days of wretchedness and uncertainty in that busy port, where he could not get rid of the idea that even yet he might be betrayed and sent back to Japan, our adventurer found another American vessel, the *Wild Rover*, bound for Boston, and succeeded in persuading the captain to take him on board without wages as his own personal servant. The voyage was a tedious one, for the *Wild Rover* was a "tramp," which sailed here and there about the China seas for eight months before turning homewards, and spent four months more on the ocean passage. While they were lying in Hong-Kong harbour Neesima discovered a Chinese New Testament in a shop, and felt that he must secure it at all costs. But he had not a copper of his own, and having promised to work his passage without wages, felt that he could not ask the captain for any money. At last he bethought himself of his sword, which, being a *samurai*, he had brought with him as a matter of course. Could he honourably part with this weapon which marked the dignity of his caste, and was to him like his shield to a young Spartan—an indispensable badge of his own relf-respect? He was not long in deciding. The Japanese sword was soon in the hands of a dealer, and Neesima triumphantly bore his prize back to the ship. He read the book day and night, and found in it answers to some of the questions which had so long perplexed his mind.

When the *Wild Rover* reached Boston our hero's trials were by no means over. The Civil War had lately ended. Work was scarce; the price of everything was high. Nobody wanted this Japanese lad with his "pidgin" English and his demand to be sent to school. He began to fear that the hopes of years might only have been delusions after all. "I could not read book very cheerfully," he remarks, "and I am only looking around myself a long time as a lunatic."

It is quite characteristic of his romantic experiences that his first real comfort came from a copy of *Robinson Crusoe* which he picked up for a few cents in a second-hand bookstore. Possibly he felt that there were some analogies between his adventures and trials and those of the hero of Defoe's great romance, and that he was almost as friendless and solitary on the shores of this great continent as the shipwrecked mariner on that lonely island beach. But what appealed to him most of all was Crusoe's prayers. Hitherto he had cried to God as an unknown God, feeling all the while that perhaps God had no eyes to see him, no ears to listen for him. Now he learned from Crusoe's manner of praying that in all his troubles he must cry to God as a present, personal friend. And so day by day, in the full belief that God was listening, he uttered this prayer "Please don't cast me away into miserable condition. Please let me reach my great aim."

Neesima's worst anxieties were nearly over now. His "great aim" was almost in sight. As soon as the *Wild Rover* reached Boston, the captain had gone off on a long visit to his friends, not thinking much about his Japanese cabin-boy or expecting to see him again. But on his return to his ship some weeks after, he found "Joe," as the lad was called on shipboard, still hovering about the vessel as his one ark of refuge. This led him to speak to his owner, a Mr. Hardy, of the queer young Oriental he had brought to America; and Mr. Hardy, who was a large-hearted and generous Christian man, at once declared that he would make some provision for the poor fellow. His first idea was to employ him as a house servant; but when his wife and he met the youth and heard his wonderful story, they saw immediately that this was no ordinary immigrant of the stowaway order; and instead of making him a servant they took him into their family practically as an adopted son, and gave him a thorough education, first in an academy at Andover and afterwards at Amherst College. It was in token of this adoption that, when he was baptized as a member of the Christian Church, he took his full name of Joseph Hardy Neesima. On shipboard, as has been mentioned, he was called "Joe," the sailors having decided that he must have some short and handy name, and "Joe" suggesting itself as convenient. "Keep the name," Mr. Hardy said after hearing how it was given. For he felt that, like another Joseph, who went down to Egypt as a captive and became the saviour of his brethren, Joseph

Neesima, the Japanese runaway, might yet become a benefactor to his country. He lived long enough to see his hopes much more than realized.

After graduating honourably at Amherst College, Neesima entered himself a student at Andover Theological Seminary, with the view of being ordained as a fully qualified missionary to his own countrymen. Soon after this a pathway for his return to Japan opened up in a manner which was almost dramatic. Since his departure from Hakodate in 1864, the chariot wheels of progress had been moving rapidly in the land of his birth. Japan was beginning to deserve in a wider sense than before its name of "The Land of the Rising Sun." Instead of closing all her doors and windows and endeavouring to shut out the light at every chink, she was now eager to live and move in the full sunshine of Western knowledge. The great political and social revolution had taken place. The Mikado had issued that epoch-making proclamation in which he declared: "The uncivilized customs of former times will be broken; the impartiality and justice displayed in the workings of nature adopted as a basis of action; and intellect and learning will be sought for throughout the world in order to establish the foundations of empire."

It was in pursuance of this new policy that there came to Washington in the winter of 1871-72 a distinguished embassy from the Imperial Court of Japan, which had for its special commission to inspect and report upon the workings of Western civilization. The embassy soon felt the need of some one who could not only act as interpreter, but assist it in the task of examining the institutions, and especially the educational institutions, of foreign lands. For some time Mr. Mori, the Japanese Minister in the United States, had had his eye on his young countryman at Andover, and he now invited him to Washington to be introduced to the embassy. So favourable was the impression produced by his personal appearance, and so evident was it that he was thoroughly conversant with the principles and methods of Western culture, that he was immediately requested to accompany the ambassadors in the capacity of adviser, on their tour through the United States and Europe; while overtures of the most flattering kind were made to him, with brilliant prospects in the political world whenever he returned to his native land. But Neesima's mind was now fully made up regarding his work in life. When he returned to Japan it would be not as a politician, but as a Christian missionary. In the meantime, however, he willingly put his services at the disposal of the Mikado's embassy, and thereby not only greatly enlarged his experience, but gained influential friends among the rising statesmen of Japan, friends who were afterwards of no small help to him in his efforts to promote among his countrymen the cause of a Christian civilization. The special task was assigned to him of drawing up a paper on "The Universal Education of Japan." He discharged the duty with such ability that his essay became the basis of the report subsequently made by the embassy on the subject of education. And this report, with certain modifications, was the foundation of the Japanese system of education as it has existed ever since.

After a year had been spent in this interesting way,

NEESIMA'S EDUCATIONAL DREAMS

Neesima returned to Andover, and on the completion of his theological course was ordained by the American Board of Missions as an evangelist to his fellow-countrymen, his foster-father, Mr. Hardy, undertaking to provide for his support. Ten years had now elapsed from the time when he was smuggled out of Japan in the hold of a little schooner—a poor and unknown lad, and a criminal in the eyes of the law. He was about to return a highly cultured Christian gentleman, with not a few influential friends on both sides of the Pacific. And he was returning with a purpose. He had found the light he came to seek, but he was far from being satisfied with that. His aim now was to be a light-bringer to Japan. He was deeply conscious of the truth that

> Heaven doth with us as we with torches do,
> Not light them for themselves.

He was unwilling, says Dr. Davis, his colleague in after years and one of his biographers, "to go back with a full heart but with an empty hand." His purpose was to start a Christian College in which he could meet the craving of Young Japan for Western knowledge—the craving which he knew so well—while at the same time he might surround the students with a Christian atmosphere, and train some of them to be preachers and teachers of Jesus Christ. But he could not start a college without means, and where the means were to come from he did not know.

He spoke of his plans in the first place to various members of the American Board. But the Board's hands were full, and he met with no encouragement. Then he took counsel with himself. It had been arranged that before leaving America he should give an address at the annual public meeting of the Board, and he determined to utilize this opportunity. To the very best of his ability he prepared a speech. But when he stepped on to the platform and faced the great audience, a fate befell him which has often come to public speakers at a critical moment in the beginning of their careers. His carefully arranged ideas all disappeared; his mind became a perfect blank; and every one present thought that he had completely broken down. But suddenly a thought flashed into his mind, opening up an entirely fresh line of address, and for fifteen minutes, while the tears streamed down his cheeks, he pleaded the cause of his country with such overwhelming earnestness that at the close of his short speech 5000 dollars were subscribed on the spot, and Neesima knew that the foundation-stone of a Christian College in Japan was already laid.

It was characteristic of our hero's indomitable courage that when he reached Japan he started his college, which he called the "Doshisha," or "Company of One Endeavour" —not in any city of the coast, where Western ideas had become familiar, but in Kyoto itself, the sacred city of the interior, a city of 6000 temples and the very heart of the religious life of Old Japan. In this place, where Buddhism and Shintoism had flourished unchallenged for a thousand years, Neesima was subjected for a time to the furious hatred of the native priests and even to the opposition of the magistrates. For the most part these men had no objections to Western education, but Christian education they would have liked to suppress. It was now that he realized the advantage of the friendship of the members of the embassy of 1871-2. Several of those gentlemen, including the present Marquis Ito, had become prominent members of the Japanese Cabinet, and they did not a little to remove difficulties out of Neesima's way.

And so the Doshisha took root and flourished, until in the last year of its founder's life, when he had been engaged in his work for fifteen years, the number of students in all departments, young women as well as young men, had risen to over 900. Neesima wore himself out by his labours, and died at the comparatively early age of 47, just when he had taken steps to broaden out the Doshisha College into the Doshisha University, and had secured large sums for this purpose, including a single gift of 100,000 dollars from a gentleman in New England, and a collection of 31,000 yen subscribed at a dinner-party in Tokyo in the house of Count Inouye, after those present had been addressed by Neesima himself, who was one of the guests.

Neesima's widow has fulfilled his last wish, spoken from the depths of a humble Christian heart: "Raise no monument after my death. It is enough, if on a wooden cross there stands the word, 'The grave of Joseph Neesima.'" But the Doshisha is Neesima's living monument in Japan. More than 5000 students have passed through it, of whom in 1903 above eighty were preachers of the Gospel. 161 were teachers, 27 were Government officials, and 16 were newspaper editors. By turning out a succession of highly educated men and women trained under Christian influences. Neesima's college has contributed no small part in the creation of that New Japan which has so swiftly stepped in these late years into the foremost rank of the great company of nations.

The chief authority for this chapter is *A Maker of New Japan Joseph Hardy Neesima*, by Rev. J. D. Davis, D.D. (Fleming H. Revell Co.)

CHAPTER IV

"FROM FAR FORMOSA."

George Leslie Mackay—A lawless land—The Malay and the Chinaman—Dentistry and the Gospel—A cruel plot—The capture of Bang-kah—The barbarians of the plain—The Kap-tsu-lan fishermen—The mountain head-hunters—A Christmas night in a head-hunter's house.

FOR the title of this chapter we have taken the name of a book by Dr. George Leslie Mackay, of the Canadian Presbyterian Church, whose acquaintance with Formosa and its people—the people of the mountains as well as of the plains—is of an altogether unique kind. The title is appropriate, for though on the map Formosa is not more distant than China or Japan, it is much farther off than the moon to the vast majority of people, so far as any knowledge of it is concerned. Indeed, until it became a storm centre of the Chino-Japanese War of 1895, and passed under the sway of the Mikado, and was thus made an object of fresh interest to the Western world, there were numbers of fairly well-informed people who knew no more about it than that it was an island somewhere in the Eastern Seas. But more than thirty years ago it had attracted the attention of Mr. Mackay, a young Canadian of Highland Scottish descent. Sent out to China as a missionary by the Presbyterian

Church of Canada, which gave him a pretty free hand in the selection of a definite sphere, he chose the northern part of Formosa—perfectly virgin soil so far as any Christian work was concerned. The evangelization of North Formosa was a hard and dangerous task to be attempted by a single man, but Mackay flung himself into it with all the enthusiasm of a Celt, as well as the steady devotion of a brave soldier of the Church militant.

Formosa was a wild and lawless land, with its mixture of mutually hostile races, its debased Mongolians and savage Malayans, its men of the plains and men of the mountains, its corrupt officials in the towns and savage head-hunters in the hill forests. Mackay, however, went about fearlessly, with a dentist's forceps (a wonderful talisman) in one hand and a Bible in the other. At one time we find him sleeping contentedly in the filthy cabin of a farmer on the swampy rice plains with a litter of pigs, it might almost be said, for his bed-fellows, the pig being a highly domesticated animal in Formosa, and treated by its master as an Englishman treats his pet dog. Again, he is far up amongst the mountains in the land of the head-hunters, where his sleeping apartment, which is also the sleeping apartment of the whole family, is adorned with a row of grinning skulls and queues that testifies to the prowess of his host in murdering Chinamen and other dwellers on the plains. It was by a courage and persistence which nothing could daunt that this young Scoto-Canadian won his way in Formosa, until to those who are interested in the history of missions, "Mackay of Formosa" seems as natural and inevitable a title as "Mackay of Uganda" or "Chalmers of New Guinea."

Apart from the Japanese settlers who have planted themselves in the island since the war of 1895, the population of Formosa is divided between the aborigines, who are of a Malayan stock, and the Chinese, who in ever-increasing numbers have poured in from the adjacent mainland. Though only half the size of Scotland, the island is dominated by a range of mountains quite Alpine in their height, the loftiest rising to between 14,000 and 15,000 feet above the sea. Along the coast, however, there are fertile stretches, perfectly flat, formed by the alluvial deposits washed down in the course of ages. On the richer of these plains, as well as on the lower reaches of the hills, the incoming Chinamen settled, usually by no better title than the right of might. "Rice-farms and tea-plantations took the place of forest tangle and wild plateau; the rude hamlets of another race vanished; towns and cities with their unmistakable marks of the 'Middle Kingdom' took their place; and the Chinese became a superior power in Formosa."

To the Chinese, of course, the original inhabitants without exception were "barbarians," but the Malayan population, though comprising a great many different tribes, may be roughly divided into two well-defined sections. First there are those who have accepted Chinese authority, and in a modified form have adopted the Chinese civilization and religion. These go by the name of Pe-po-hoan, or "barbarians of the plain." Then there are those who have absolutely refused to acknowledge the Chinese invaders as the masters of Formosa, and, though

Dr. MacKay and his Assistants as Dentists

driven into the mountains and forests, have retained their ancestral freedom. These are the much-dreaded Chhi-hoan or "raw barbarians," whose manner of life in many respects recalls that of their kinsmen the Hill Dyaks of Borneo. Among these mountain savages, as formerly among the Dyaks, head-hunting is cultivated as a fine art. They hate the Chinese with a deadly hatred, and hardly less their own Pe-po-hoan kinsfolk who have yielded to the stranger and accepted his ways. Pe-po-hoan and Chinaman alike are considered as fair game, and their skulls are mingled indiscriminately in the ghastly collection which is the chief glory of the mountain brave, as it forms the principal adornment of his dwelling.

Naturally it was among the Chinese in the towns that Mackay began his work. He was fortunate in gathering round him very early some earnest young men, who not only accepted Christianity for themselves, but became his disciples and followers with a view to teaching and helping others. These students, as they were called, accompanied him on all his tours, not only gaining valuable experience thereby, but being of real assistance in various ways. For instance, Mackay soon discovered that the people of Formosa, partly because of the prevalence of malarial fever, and partly because they are constantly chewing the betel-nut, have very rotten teeth and suffer dreadfully from toothache. Though not a doctor, he knew a little of medicine and surgery, having attended classes in these subjects by way of preparing himself for his work abroad; but he found that nothing helped him so much in making his way among the people as his modest skill in dentistry. The priests and other enemies of Christianity might persuade the people that their fevers and other ailments had been cured not by the medicines of the "foreign devil," but by the intervention of their own gods. The power of the missionary, however, to give instantaneous relief to one in the agonies of toothache was unmistakable, and tooth-extraction worked wonders in breaking down prejudice and opposition. It was here that some of the students proved especially useful. They learned to draw teeth almost if not quite as well as Mackay himself, so that between them they were able to dispose of as many as 500 patients in an afternoon.

The usual custom of Mackay and his little band of students as they journeyed about the country was to take their stand in an open space, often on the stone steps of a temple, and after singing a hymn or two to attract attention, to proceed to the work of tooth-pulling, thereafter inviting the people to listen to their message. For the most part the crowd was very willing to listen. Sudden relief from pain produces gratitude even towards a "foreign devil," and the innate Chinese suspicion of some black arts or other evil designs was always guarded against by scrupulously placing the tooth of each patient in the palm of his own hand. The people began to love Mackay, and this opened their hearts to his preaching. Men and women came to confess their faith, and in one large village which was the centre of operations there were so many converts that a preaching-hall had to be secured, which Sunday after Sunday was packed by an expectant crowd.

Opposition is often the best proof of success, and in Mackay's case it soon came in cruel and tragic forms. A cunning plot was laid between the priestly party and the civil officials to accuse a number of these Chinese Christians of conspiring to assassinate the mandarin. Six innocent men were seized and put in the stocks in the dungeons of the city of Bang-kah. Mock trials were held, in the course of which the prisoners were bambooed, made to kneel on red-hot chains, and tortured in various other ways. At last one morning two of the heroic band, a father and son, were taken out of their dungeon and dragged off to the place of execution. The son's head was chopped off before his father's eyes, after which the old man too was put to death. Then their heads, placed in baskets, were carried slowly back to Bang-kah with the notice fixed above them, *Jip kon-e lang than* ("Heads of the Christians"). All along the way the town-crier summoned the multitude to witness the fate of those who followed the "barbarian". And when the walls of Bang-kah were reached the two heads were fastened above the city gate, just as the heads of criminals or martyrs used to be set above the Netherbow at Edinburgh or Temple Bar in London, for a terror and a warning to all who passed by. It was a cruel fate, and yet better than that of the remaining prisoners. Their lot was to be slowly starved or tortured to death in their filthy dungeons.

But in spite of these horrors—partly, we might say, because of them—the number of Christians in North Formosa steadily grew, until at length, as Dr. Mackay puts it, "Bang-kah itself was taken." Not that this important place, "the Gibraltar of heathendom" in the island, was transformed into a Christian city. But it ceased, at all events, to be fiercely anti-Christian, and came to honour the very man whom it had hustled, hooted at, pelted with mud and rotten eggs, and often plotted to kill. A striking proof of the change was given by and by when Mackay was about to return to Canada on a visit. The head men of the city sent a deputation to ask him to allow them to show their appreciation of himself and his work by according him a public send-off. He was not sure about it at first, not caring much for demonstrations of this kind, but on reflection concluded that it might be well, and might do good to the Christian cause, to allow them to have their own way. So he was carried through the streets of Bang-kah to the jetty in a silk-lined sedan-chair, preceded by the officials of the place, and followed by three hundred soldiers and bands of civilians bearing flags and banners, to a musical accompaniment provided by no fewer than eight Chinese orchestras made up of cymbals, drums, gongs, pipes, guitars, mandolines, tambourines, and clarionets. Heathens and Christians alike cheered him as he boarded the steam-launch which was to take him off from the shore, while the Christians who had stood firmly by him through troublous times broke into a Chinese version of the old Scottish paraphrase, "I'm not ashamed to own my Lord."

But while Mackay found his base of operations among the Chinese in the north and west of Formosa, he did not forget the Malayan aborigines, whether those of the plains or those of the mountains. As soon as he had got a firm footing and gathered a band of competent helpers around him, he began to turn his attention to the Pe-po-hoan, the "barbarians of the plain," who cultivate their rice-farms in the low-lying and malarial districts along the north-east coast. He had already experienced many of the drawbacks of Formosan travel. He had known what it was to be swept down the current in trying to ford dangerous streams, to push his way through jungles full of lurking serpents, to encounter hostile crowds in village or town who jeered at the "foreign devil," or regarded him, as the boy said of birds in his essay on the subject, as being "very useful to throw stones at." And night when it came he had often found not less trying than day, possibly still more so. The filthy rest-houses were not places of much rest to a white man. Pigs frisked out and in, and slept or grunted beneath the traveller's bed. The bed itself was a plank with brick legs, the mattress a dirty grass mat on which coolies had smoked opium for years. And when, overpowered by weariness, he fell asleep, he was apt to be suddenly awakened by the attacks of what he humorously describes as "three generations of crawling creatures."

Greater dangers and worse discomforts than these, however, had now to be faced in carrying the Gospel to the country of the Pe-po-hoan. In the mountains over which it was necessary to pass in order to cross from the west coast to the east, Mackay and his students had to run the gauntlet of the stealthy head-hunters. They had more than one narrow escape. Passing by the mouth of a gorge one day, they heard in the distance blood-curdling yells and screams, and presently a Chinese came rushing up all out of breath and told them that he and four others had just been attacked by the savages, and that his companions were all speared and beheaded, while he had only managed to escape with his life. When the plains were reached the Pe-po-hoan did not prove at first a friendly or receptive people. From village after village they were turned away with reviling, the inhabitants often setting their wolfish dogs upon them. The weather was bad, and in that low-lying region the roads were soon turned into quagmires where the feet sank into eighteen inches of mud. When night fell a Chinese inn would have been welcome enough; but sometimes no better sleeping-place could be had than the lee side of a dripping rice-stack.

But after a while things began to improve. Like Jesus in Galilee, Mackay found his first disciples in the Kap-tsu-lan plain among the fishermen—bold, hardy fellows, who live in scattered villages along that coast. Three of these fishers came to him one day and said, "You have been going through and through our plain, and no one has received you. Come to our village, and we will listen to you." They led Mackay and his students to their village, gave them a good supper of rice and fish, and then one of them took a large conch shell, which in other days had served as a war-trumpet, and summoned the whole population to an assembly. Till the small hours of the morning Mackay was kept busy preaching, conversing, discussing, and answering questions. The very next day these people determined to have a church of their own in which to worship the true God. They sailed down the coast to the forest country farther south to cut logs of wood, and though they were attacked by the savages while doing so, and some of them wounded, they returned in due course with a load of timber. Bricks were made out of mud and rice-chaff, and a primitive little chapel was soon erected, in which every evening at the blowing of the conch the entire village met to hear the preacher. Mackay stayed two months in this place, and by that time it had become nominally Christian. Several times, he tells us, he dried his dripping clothes at night in front of a fire made of idolatrous paper, idols, and ancestral tablets which the people had given him to destroy. One reason for this rapid and wholesale conversion to Christianity no doubt lay in the fact that the Chinese idolatry which these Pe-po-hoan fishermen had been induced to accept never came very near to their hearts. Originally they or their fathers had been nature-worshippers, as all the mountain savages still are, and many of them were inclined to look upon the rites and ceremonies to which they submitted as unwelcome reminders of their subjection to an alien race.

What took place in this one village was soon repeated in several others on the Kap-tsu-lan plain. Even in places where men, women, and children had rejected him at first and hurled "the contumelious stone" at his head, Mackay came to be welcomed by the people as their best friend. And by and by no fewer than nineteen chapels sprang up in that plain, the preachers and pastors in every case being native Christians, and several of them being drawn from among the Pe-po-hoan themselves.

But something must now be said about the Chhi-hoan, or savage barbarians of the mountains. More than once in the course of his tours among the Pe-po-hoan Mackay narrowly escaped from the spears and knives of these warriors, who live by hunting wild animals in the primeval forests, but whose peculiar delight it is to hunt for human heads, and above all for the heads of the hated Chinese.

On one occasion a party of Chinese traders with whom he was staying in an outpost settlement was attacked by a band of two dozen savages; and though the latter were eventually beaten off, it was not till they had secured the heads of three of Mackay's trading friends.

According to the unwritten law of the mountain villages, no man is permitted to marry until he has proved his prowess by bringing at least one head to his chief, while eminence in the estimation of the tribe always depends upon the number of skulls which a brave can display under the eaves or along the inside walls of his hut. Mackay tells of one famous chief who was captured at last by the Chinese authorities, and who said, as he was led out to execution, that he was not ashamed to die, because in his house in the mountains he could show a row of skulls only six short of a hundred.

A head-hunter's outfit consists, in the first place, of a long, light thrusting-spear with an arrow-shaped blade eight inches in length. In his belt he carries a cruel-looking crooked knife with which to slash off his victim's head. Over the shoulder he wears a bag of strong, twisted twine, capable of carrying two or three heads at a time. From the attacks of these bloodthirsty savages none who live or move on the borderland between mountain and plain are ever secure by day or by night. In the daytime the hunters usually go out singly, concealing themselves in the tall grass of the level lands, or behind some stray boulder by a path through a glen along which sooner or later a traveller is likely to pass. When his quarry is within spear-thrust, the crouching hunter leaps upon him, striking for his heart; and soon a headless corpse is lying on the

ARMED HEAD-HUNTERS IN FORMOSA

Their victims are men, Chinese or even their own people who have been conquered and live amongst the Chinese. Their outfit consists of a spear, a knife, and a bag capable of holding two or three heads. No sleuth-hound is truer to the scent, no tiger stealthier of foot in the pursuit of prey.

ground, while the savage, with his prize slung round his neck, is trotting swiftly, by forest paths known only to himself, towards his distant mountain home.

But more commonly the attack is made at night, and made by a party of braves. In this case everything is carefully planned for weeks before. Watchers on the hill-tops, or scouts lurking in the bush along the edge of the forests, report as to when a village festivity is likely to make its defenders less watchful, or when the fishermen have gone off on a distant fishing expedition, leaving their homes to the care of none but womenfolk. Having selected a house for attack, the savages silently surround it in the darkness, creeping stealthily nearer and nearer until, at a signal from the leader, one of them moves on before the rest and sets fire to the thatch. When the unfortunate inmates, aroused from sleep by the crackle of the flames and half-stifled by the smoke, attempt to rush out of the door, they are instantly speared and their heads secured. In a few moments, before the nearest neighbours have had time to come to the rescue, or even been awakened from their slumbers, the hunters have disappeared into the night.

The return to the village of a successful head-hunting party is a scene of fiendish delight, in which men, women, and children alike all take a part. Hour after hour dancing and drinking is carried on, as the Chhi-hoan gloat over the death of their enemies and praise the prowess of their warriors. On rare occasions the heads of the victims are boiled and the flesh eaten, but it is quite common to boil the brain to a jelly and eat it with the gusto of revenge. Dr. Mackay has bimself been present in a mountain village on the return of a head-hunting party, and has been offered some of this brain jelly as a rare treat.

One who goes among such people must literally take his life in his hands, for he may at any moment fall a victim to treachery or to the inherited passion for human blood. But perfect courage and unvarying truth and kindness will carry a traveller far, and Mackay had the further advantage of being possessed of medical and surgical skill. He owed something, moreover, to his *not* having a pigtail. "You must be a kinsman of ours," the Chhi-hoan said, as they examined the missionary's back hair. And so by degrees Mackay came to live in close touch with these savages, and found that, apart from their head-hunting instincts, they had some good and amiable qualities of their own. From time to time he visited them as he got opportunity, and was even able in some cases to bring a measure of light to very benighted minds.

One year Mackay spent a Christmas holiday high up among the mountains as the guest of one of the barbarian chiefs. The house was a single large room, fully thirty feet long, in which at night a fire blazed at either end. Around one fire the women squatted spinning cord for nets, around the other the braves smoked and discussed a head-hunting expedition which they proposed to undertake before long. On the walls were the customary rows of skulls, their grinning teeth lighted up fitfully by the flickering gleams from the burning fir logs. In the midst of this promiscuous crowd, which included a mother and her newborn babe, Mackay with his students had to sleep that night. But before the time came to lie down and rest, he proposed that he and his Christian companions should give a song, a proposal which secured silence at once, for the aborigines are much more musical than the Chinese, and are very fond of singing. And so on Christmas night, in that wild spot where no white man had ever been before, and to that strange audience, Mackay and his little band of Chinese converts sang some Christian hymns. And after that he told the listening savages the story of the first Christmas night, and of the love of Him who was born in the stable at Bethlehem for the head-hunters of Formosa, no less than for the white men whose home was over the sea.

NOTE.—The material for this chapter is derived from Dr. Mackay's book, *From Far Formosa* (Edinburgh: Oliphant, Anderson, and Ferrier).

CHAPTER V

A HEROINE OF TIBET

Mysterious Lhasa—The lady who tried to lift the veil—In the Himalayas—On the Chino-Tibetan frontier—The caravan for Lhasa—Attacked by brigands—The kilted Goloks—Among perpetual snows—A Tibetan love story—Noga the traitor—The arrest—Return to China—In the Chumbi Valley.

WHEN an armed British expedition struggled over the Karo-la Pass, which exceeds Mont Blanc in height, and entered Lhasa on the 3rd of August, 1904, there was a brief lifting of the veil of mystery which has hung for centuries around the city of the Grand Lama. But the wreathing snows, which began to fall so heavily around the little army before it reached the frontiers of India on the return journey, were almost symbolical of the fact that Lhasa was already wrapping herself once more in her immemorial veil of cold aloofness from European eyes. Prior to the arrival of this military expedition, only one Englishman, Thomas Manning, had succeeded in reaching Lhasa, and it will soon be a century since his bold march was made. Sixty years ago two French missionary priests, the Abbés Huc and Gabet, undertook their celebrated journey from China to Lhasa, which they afterwards described in a very interesting book. But though they reached their goal, they gained little by it, for they were soon deported back to China again. No Protestant missionary has ever set foot in Lhasa, and what is more, no Protestant missionary, with one exception, has ever made a determined attempt to reach it. And to the honour of her sex be it said, the one who made the attempt and all but succeeded was a lady, and a lady with no other following than a couple of faithful Asiatic servants.

The character and career of Miss Annie R. Taylor remind one at some points of the late General Gordon. There is the same shrinking from public notice, the same readiness to be buried from the sight of Europe in some distant and difficult task, the same courage which fears nothing, the same simple, unquestioning trust in the care and guidance of a heavenly Father. Miss Taylor went out to China in 1884 in the service of the China Inland Mission, and worked for some time at Tau-chau, a city which lies in the extreme north-west and quite near the Tibetan frontier. In 1887 she paid a visit to the great Lama monastery of Kum-bum, the very monastery in which MM. Huc and Gabet had stayed long before while they were learning the Tibetan language. The memory of these two adventurous priests may have stirred a spirit of imitation in a kindred heart, but what chiefly pressed upon Miss Taylor's thoughts as she stood in the Kum-bum lamasery and looked out to the west, was the vision of that great unevangelized land which stretched beyond the horizon for a thousand miles. That this land was not only shut, but almost hermetically sealed, against foreigners she knew perfectly well. But her dictionary, like Napoleon's, did not contain the word "impossible." She recalled Christ's marching orders to His Church, "Go ye into all the world!" and said to herself, "Our Lord has given us no commands which are impossible to be carried out." And if no one else was ready in Christ's name to try to scale "the roof of the world," and press on into the sacred city of Lhasa itself, she determined that she, at all events, would make the attempt.

Her first idea was to make India her point of departure, for Lhasa lies much nearer to India than to China, though the comparative shortness of this route is balanced by the fact that it leads right over the Himalayas. She went accordingly to Darjeeling, pressed on into Sikkim, which had not yet passed under British rule, and settled down near a Tibetan fort called Kambajong, with the view of mastering the language thoroughly before proceeding any farther. From the first the Tibetan suspicion of all strangers showed itself. The people would often ask her in an unpleasantly suggestive manner what they should do with her body if she died. Her answer was, that she had no intention of dying just then. The intentions of the natives, however, did not coincide with her own, and they next resorted to a custom they have of "praying people dead." Their faith in the power of prayer did not hinder them from giving Heaven some assistance in getting their prayers answered. One day the chief's wife invited Miss Taylor to dinner, and set before her an appetizing dish of rice and eggs. She had not long partaken of it when she fell seriously ill, with all the symptoms of aconite poisoning. On her recovery she wisely left this district, and settled down to live

PONTSO
Miss Taylor's servant

TAKING TEA IN TIBETAN STYLE

In the centre is Miss Taylor; at the left is Pontso, holding a leather bag of barley flour; on the right is his wife, holding the teapot. The three wooden bowls are the teacups. At the extreme right is a bamboo churn; in front of it goatskin bellows with an iron funnel; and in the centre, in front, are leather bags for tea, butter, etc.

CHURNING TEA

the life of the natives themselves in a little hut near the Tibetan monastery of Podang Gumpa.

After a year spent in this way, for ten months of which she never saw the face of a white person, she realized the impracticability of making her way to Lhasa by the Himalayan route, which is far more jealously guarded than the one from the frontiers of China. She decided, therefore, to return to China, and to make it her starting-point. Her time in Sikkim had not been wasted. In the first place, she had not only learned Tibetan thoroughly, but had acquired it in its purest form as spoken at Lhasa. In the next place, she had gained a friend and attendant who was to prove of invaluable service to her in her future wanderings. A young Tibetan named Pontso, a native of Lhasa, had met with a serious accident while travelling on the frontiers of India. Some one directed him to the white lady for treatment. He had never seen a foreigner before, but the kindness and care with which Miss Taylor nursed him in his sufferings completely won his heart. He became a believer in the religion which prompted such goodness to a stranger, devoted himself thenceforth to the service of his benefactress, and justified the trust she placed in him by his unfailing courage and fidelity.

Taking Pontso with her, Miss Taylor now sailed to Shanghai, made her way up the Yang-tse for 2,000 miles, and then on to Tau-chau on the Tibetan frontier. By way of preparing herself still further for her projected march into the interior, she visited a number of lamaseries in that region, made friends with the lamas, and learned everything she could about the Tibetan religion and ways of life and thought.

THE START FROM TAU-CHAU

About a year after her return to Tau-chau the opportunity came for which she had been waiting. Among her acquaintances in the town was a Chinese Mohammedan named Noga, whose wife, Erminie, was a Lhasa woman. Noga was a trader who had several times been to Lhasa, and on his last journey had brought away this Lhasa wife. According to a Tibetan custom, he had married her only for a fixed term, and as the three years named in the bond were now fully up, Erminie was anxious to return to her native city, and Noga quite willing to convey her back. The only question was one of ways and means, and when they found that Miss Taylor wished to go to Lhasa, Noga made a proposal. He would himself guide her all the way to the capital, provided she supplied the horses and met all necessary expenses. Miss Taylor at once agreed to his terms, which, if the Chinaman had been honest, would have been advantageous to both parties. But Noga was a deep-dyed scoundrel, as Miss Taylor soon discovered to her cost.

It was on the 2nd of September, 1892, that this brave Englishwoman set out on her heroic enterprise. She was accompanied by five Asiatics—Noga and his wife, her faithful attendant Pontso, a young Chinese whom she had engaged as an additional servant, and a Tibetan frontiersman, Nobgey by name, who asked permission to join the little company, as he also was bound for Lhasa. There were sixteen horses in the cavalcade, two mounts being provided for most of the travellers, while there were several pack-horses loaded with tents, bedding, cloth for barter, presents for chiefs, and provisions for two months.

Miss Taylor and her Party attacked by Tibetan Brigands

ATTACKED BY BRIGANDS

They had not proceeded far into the wild country which begins immediately after the Chinese frontier is left behind, when their troubles commenced. They came suddenly upon a group of eight brigands who were haunting the mountain track for the express purpose of relieving travellers of their valuables. Fortunately the brigands had not noticed their approach, and were seated round a fire enjoying the favourite Tibetan meal of tea—a meal in more senses than one, for Tibetans thicken the beverage with a handful of barley meal, so that it becomes a kind of gruel. Moreover, the robbers were armed with old-fashioned matchlocks, the tinder-boxes of which it took some time to light, and as Miss Taylor's party, though weaker in numbers, were better armed, they succeeded in beating off their assailants.

Three days after, they overtook a caravan of friendly Mongols travelling in the same direction as themselves, and in view of their recent experience, thought it wise to amalgamate their forces. Their satisfaction at being thus reinforced was not long-lived. Almost immediately after a band of brigands 200 strong swept down upon the caravan, entirely surrounded it, and began firing from all sides. Two men were killed and seven wounded; resistance was hopeless, and the whole company had to surrender. The Mongols and Nobgey were robbed of everything, and had to turn back; but as the brigand code of honour forbids war upon women, Miss Taylor and her four attendants were allowed to pass on their way, not, however, without being deprived of two of the horses and a good part of the luggage.

The next stage of the journey lay through the land of

a strange people known as the Goloks. This is a fierce and warlike race, bearing some resemblance both in habits and dress to the Scotch Highlanders of other days. They draw up their sheepskin garments by a girdle so as to form a kind of kilt, and leave their knees bare, while covering the lower part of their limbs with cloth leggings fastened with garters of bright-coloured wool. Like the Highlanders of long ago, they have a great contempt for law and authority, and acknowledge neither Tibetan nor Chinese rule. The chief delight of their lives is to engage in forays upon people of more peaceful tastes and habits than themselves. Issuing in large bodies from their mountain glens under some fighting chieftain, they sweep down upon the people of some neighbouring tribe, and carry off as booty their cattle, horses, sheep, tents, and other belongings. Among the Goloks Miss Taylor would have fared even worse than she had already done at the hands of the brigands, but for the fact that the part of the tribe with which she first came in contact was ruled by a chieftainess, a woman named Wachu Bumo. On discovering that this white traveller was also a woman, Wachu Bumo took quite a fancy to her, and not only saw to it that she was treated courteously so long as she remained in the Golok valleys, but insisted on furnishing her with an escort of two Golok horsemen to see her safely on her way for some distance after she had left the country of these marauders.

It is characteristic of Miss Taylor that in her little book, *Pioneering in Thibet*, she says hardly anything about her own hardships and sufferings in that long march through one of the wildest regions of the world.

For a great part of the way, it must be remembered, the route ran among mountains covered with perpetual snow. Rivers had to be crossed which knew neither bridge nor ferry nor ford. Winter too was coming on, and they had often to advance in the teeth of blinding storms of sleet and snow. In England Miss Taylor had been considered delicate, but a brave spirit and a strong will carried her through experiences which might well have broken down the strongest physique. Shortly after they had left the land of the Goloks the cold and exposure proved too much for her Chinese servant, a tall, powerful young man. Miss Taylor does not dwell upon the circumstances of his death, but a glimpse like the following is suggestive by its very reticence: "We buried him at noon. A bright sun lightened up the snow-clad hills when the men dug up a few hard sods in some swampy ground close by, laid down the body in its shroud of white cotton cloth, and covered it as best they could with the frost-bound earth. At night the wolves were howling round the grave. This was in the Peigo country."

In a little mountain town called Gala Miss Taylor made the interesting acquaintance of a couple, Pa-tegn and Per-ma, whose marriage had a flavour of romance unusual in Tibet. From infancy Pa-tegn had been dedicated to the priesthood, and had been brought up accordingly in a lamasery. But when about twenty years of age he suddenly fell in love with Per-ma. The course of his true love could not possibly run smooth, for celibacy is as binding on a Buddhist lama as on a Romish priest. But "one fine day," as Miss

Taylor puts it, "this Tibetan Abelard disappeared, and in company with Per-ma made his way to Lhasa." Here he discarded his priest's robe and became a tailor. After a child had been born to them they decided to return to Gala, and by means of a judicious present succeeded in soothing the outraged feelings of the local chief. In the house of this couple Miss Taylor stayed for some time to rest from her fatigues, and when she was setting out again persuaded Pa-tegn, who was an experienced traveller and knew Lhasa well, to come with her in place of the Chinese attendant she had recently lost. It was fortunate for her that she secured his services. He proved a capable and devoted follower, and it would have gone ill with her, as she soon found out, but for his presence and help.

They were now in the very heart of the mountains, and Noga, the Chinese guide, feeling that Miss Taylor was thoroughly in his power, began to appear in his true character. Both he and his wife had behaved very badly from the first, but it now became evident that his real purpose all along had been to rob and murder his employer before reaching Lhasa. More than once he made deliberate attempts on her life, but on each occasion the vigilance of Pontso and Pa-tegn defeated his villainy; and at last he contented himself with deserting her altogether, carrying off at the same time, along with his wife, a horse, a mule, and the larger of the two tents.

The little party of three—Miss Taylor and two Tibetans—was now reduced to such straits for lack of food that the only remaining tent had to be bartered for the necessaries of life; and though it was now the middle of December in that awful climate, they had henceforth to sleep in the open air. When night fell they looked about for holes in the ground, so that they might have a little shelter from the high and piercing winds which in those elevated regions are constantly blowing. A march of several days brought them to the Dam-jau-er-la Pass, one of the loftiest and most dreaded passes in Tibet. Here the cold is so paralysing that it is not uncommon for some travellers in a caravan to be completely overpowered by it, so that they drop down helpless by the wayside. There they are simply left to perish, since any halt on their account might mean death to others of the company.

At length the waters of the Bo-Chu were crossed, the boundary of the sacred province of Ü, in which Lhasa stands, and the goal of the journey seemed almost in sight. But alas for their hopes! In the middle of a deep gorge through which the path ran, two fully armed Tibetan soldiers sprang out from behind the rocks, ordered them to halt, and took them prisoners. This was on January 3rd, 1893. Miss Taylor soon learned to what this arrest was due. Noga, after deserting her, had hurried on in front for the purpose of lodging information that he had met two Tibetans conducting a European lady towards Lhasa. Guards were accordingly placed at all the approaches, and Miss Taylor had walked into a prepared trap. For several days she was kept a prisoner, surrounded by about twenty soldiers, and having no better shelter by day or night than a narrow coffin-shaped hole in the ground. At last she and her two attendants were brought before some chiefs who had been summoned from

Lhasa, and a trial was entered into which lasted for days, communication with the capital being kept up all the while by special messengers. Word came from Lhasa that the white lady was to be treated courteously, and this injunction was carefully attended to. But the issue of the trial was never in doubt. When only three days' march from the Sacred City, nearer than any of the later European travellers had succeeded in getting, Miss Taylor had to turn back and retrace every step of the weary way from the frontiers of China.

The return was even more trying than the advance, not only because hope was now turned to disappointment, but because winter in all its rigour now lay upon the land. The Tibetan authorities, though firm, were not unkind, and supplied Miss Taylor with provisions, some money, and two horses. But the Tibetan climate made up for any gentleness on the part of the Lhasa chiefs. The cold was almost unspeakable, and the food they tried to cook over their dung fires had often to be eaten half raw and little more than half warm, since at the great elevations of the mountain passes water boiled with very little heat. For twenty days at a stretch they had to sleep on the ground in the open air, the snow falling around them all the while; for tent they had none, and there was no sign of any human habitation. Their greatest difficulty, however, was to keep their horses from starving in that frozen land. In Tibet the emergency ration for horses in winter is raw goat's flesh, which they eat greedily; but Miss Taylor could not afford to buy goats. All that could be spared to the poor steeds was a little tea with cheese and butter stirred into it, with the result that the famishing animals ate the woollen clothing of their riders whenever they got a chance.

Miss Taylor reached China safely once more, seven months and ten days after she had set out for Lhasa from the city of Tau-chau. She made no further attempt to penetrate to the Sacred City. The very year (1893) which witnessed the discomfiture of her heroic effort was marked by the signing of the Sikkim-Tibet Convention, which secured a trade-mart at Yatung, on the Tibetan side of the Indian frontier, open to all British subjects for the purposes of trade. In this political event Miss Taylor's discerning eye saw a missionary opportunity. From China she returned once more to the Himalayas, and started her remarkable mission at Yatung, in the Chumbi Valley, where by and by she secured the assistance of two other ladies—Miss Ferguson and Miss Foster. Nominally she is a trader, this being the ground of her right to settle down within the borders of the Forbidden Empire, and in point of fact she carries on some trade with the people of the district, who much prefer her dealings to those of the Chinese merchants and officials. But first of all, as both Chinese and Tibetans know, she is a missionary, partly to the bodies (for her mission is provided with a dispensary), but above all to the souls of her beloved Tibetans. "The trading is not a hardship," she writes. "If Paul could make tents for Christ, surely we can do this for our Master. So those who are 'called' to work for Tibet must be prepared for the present to sell goods to the Tibetans or attend to their ailments, as well as preach the Gospel to them." Seldom surely in the annals of Christian missions has there been a more romantic figure than that of this heroine of Tibet, who nearly succeeded in reaching Lhasa, but having failed, turned, with a sanctified common sense which might almost be described as apostolic, to the open door offered by the trading regulations of the Sikkim-Tibet Convention of 1893.

The story of Miss Taylor's march upon Lhasa, together with some account of her pioneer mission in the Chumbi Valley, will be found in her book, *Pioneering in Tibet* (London : Morgan and Scott).

CHAPTER VI

"THE SAVIOUR OF LIAO-YANG"

A medical missionary's power—The Boxer madness—The avenging Russians—Looting of Hai-cheng—The "Free Healing Hall"—In front of Liao-yang—"A fine thing done by a white man all alone"—"The Saviour of Liao-yang"—Russo-Japanese war—Battle of Liao-yang—A Mission hospital in the hour of battle—Mr. Bennet Burleigh's testimony—A robber's point of view—Adventure with bandits.

IN an earlier chapter on the work of Dr. Chamberlain among the Telugus of south-eastern India, something was said about the romantic aspects of even the ordinary routine of medical missions. Whether in the wards of his hospital or itinerating among scattered villages, the missionary doctor has an opportunity and an influence beyond any possessed by one who is only a preacher or teacher.

Jesus Christ, it has been said, was the first medical missionary. As He went about Galilee doing good, He not only "preached the Gospel of the kingdom," but "healed all manner of sickness and all manner of disease among the people." In this combination of healing with preaching lay a large part of the secret of our Lord's attractive power. The modern missionary doctor cannot work miracles. But through the progress of medical science he has acquired a marvellous power to heal sickness and relieve suffering. And by the quiet exercise of his skill amongst a heathen and sometimes hostile population, he inspires a confidence and calls forth a gratitude by which the solid walls of prejudice are rapidly broken down and locked doors are thrown wide open for the entrance of the Christian Gospel.

It is the gracious work of healing, steadily carried on from year to year, that lays the foundations of a medical missionary's power. But sometimes in the history of a mission there come hours of crisis which bring with them the chance of doing something heroic, and in which a strong man's grandest qualities become revealed. It was in such an hour that Dr. A. Macdonald Westwater, a Scotch Presbyterian missionary, gained the name of "The Saviour of Liao-yang," by which he is now known all over Manchuria.

The Boxer madness had swept up to Manchuria from the south, and had raged across the country with the swift destructiveness of a prairie fire. Hordes of Chinese soldiers joined the anti-foreign movement, and everywhere there was "red ruin and the breaking up of laws." Christian missions and native Christians suffered most, for they had to bear the full brunt of the savage hatred stirred up against the "foreign devils." But the rioters did not stop short with massacring Christians and destroying mission property. Boxerism soon turned to indiscriminate brigandage. And by and by the great city of Mukden, the capital of the three provinces of Manchuria, was looted, while for a distance of 500 miles the marauders marched along the railway line, tearing up the rails, destroying stations, plundering and burning houses and villas on either hand.

But the avengers were soon on the trail. Russian troops were poured into Manchuria, and a terrible work of reprisal was begun. Advancing simultaneously from south and north, the Russians simply wiped out every village in which they found any railway material, and left the country behind them black and smoking on both sides of what had once been the railway line.

The terror of their name travelled before them. As they drew near to Hai-cheng the people fled *en masse*, though the better-off among them, in the hope of securing some consideration for their property, took the precaution of leaving caretakers behind in their houses and shops. But the troops of the Czar treated Hai-cheng as they had already treated many a meaner place. Of the numerous caretakers left in the city only six escaped from the pitiless massacre that followed the military occupation. Hai-cheng itself was looted and left absolutely bare. And then the Russians moved onwards, still destroying as they went, and making their way now towards the important city of Liao-yang.

In Liao-yang, previous to the Boxer outbreak, a splendid work had been carried on for years by Dr. Westwater, an agent of the United Presbyterian, now the United Free Church of Scotland. His "Free Healing Hall," as the name of his mission hospital ran in Chinese, had become a place of note in the city. In this hall, as one of the citizens, not himself a Christian, expressed it, "the blind saw, the lame walked, the deaf heard; and all were counselled to virtue."

IN FRONT OF LIAO-YANG

Compelled by the Boxer fury to lay down his work in Liao-yang for a time, the doctor sought and obtained permission to accompany the Russian punitive field force as a member of the Russian Red Cross Society with General Alexandrovski at its head. He was present in every battle fought during the campaign, and immensely impressed the Russian officers by his surgical skill, which quite surpassed that of any doctor of their own. In this way he gained the good opinion and respect of the general in command, and was able to do something towards checking the frightful excesses of which, at first, the army was guilty.

When the advancing troops reached Liao-yang, a small engagement was fought in which the Chinese were defeated. Following up their victory, the Russians were just about to enter the suburbs, when they were fired upon from the city walls and so brought to a halt. Meanwhile from the Korean Gate the inhabitants were pouring out in crowds, endeavouring to make good their escape before the Russians should take the city. Numbers of people were trampled to death in the panic-stricken rush, many were pushed into the river and drowned. To crown the horrors of the scene, the Russian gunners got on to this black mass of struggling fugitives, and began to throw shells into the thick of it.

It now seemed certain that Liao-yang would share the fate that had already befallen Hai-cheng—the fate of being deserted by a terrified population and given up to massacre and loot at the hands of native brigands as well as of Russian troops. Only one man stood between it and destruction, but that man had the soul of a hero. and proved himself equal to the occasion.

Before the general had ordered an assault upon the city, Dr. Westwater had obtained an interview with him. His words were brief but to the point. "I undertake," he said, "to enter Liao-yang by myself, and to persuade the people to surrender peacefully, but upon one condition." "What is that?" asked the general. "That I have your solemn word of honour that no harm shall be done to the person of man or woman within the walls, and that there shall be absolutely no looting."

To a Russian commander this was a new way of dealing with an obstinate Chinese town. But Dr. Westwater's personality by this time had made a strong impression on him, and he at once gave his word of honour to observe the stipulated terms. The doctor then mounted his pony, and rode on all alone towards the walls of this lately Boxerised city.

Obtaining entrance by one of the gates, and riding on through the streets, he could see no sign of any living creature. It looked at first as if the whole population had already vanished, though most of them, he afterwards found, had simply shut themselves up within their houses. At last a Christian schoolboy approached who had recognized him and come out to meet him. From this boy Dr. Westwater learned that at that very time the members of the Guild—the City Fathers of Liao-yang, as they might be called—were gathered together to take counsel regarding the city's fate.

Riding on, he came to their hall of meeting, and introduced himself as one whom most of them knew as a Christian doctor, but who was now come as an ambassador of peace from the head of the Russian army. And when he went on to inform them that the general had passed his deliberate word of honour to himself to do no harm to the place if it was quietly surrendered, a thrill of astonishment and relief ran through the meeting. The word was quickly carried through the streets, and the confidence of the city was restored as if by magic. The people no longer thought of abandoning Liao-yang to its fate, but prepared with perfect calmness to receive their conquerors.

The Russian general, on the other hand, was absolutely loyal to his word. To secure that his promises should be observed to the letter he appointed, not sergeants merely, but commissioned officers to go about the streets with the patrols. And this was the altogether unexampled result. During the whole of the Russian occupation of Liao-yang there was not a single instance of crime committed by the soldiery against the person or property of any inhabitant of the city.

This gallant deed of the Scotch missionary doctor has been described by Mr. Whigham, the well-known Eastern traveller and war correspondent, as "a fine thing done by a white man all alone," and as the bravest deed of which he knows.[1] And it was this that gained for Dr. Westwater from the people of Manchuria his enviable name of "The Saviour of Liao-yang."

Upon the citizens of Liao-yang itself Dr. Westwater's action made a very deep impression. They felt that to him they owed the salvation of their lives and homes. On his return to the city after the conclusion of his period of service with the Red Cross Society, the heads of the native guilds called on him to express their gratitude. They

[1] See *The Bravest Deed I Ever Saw* (Hutchinson and Co.), p. 37.

offered him the choice of a number of compounds for a temporary house and hospital, stating their readiness to pay all the expenses of alterations, rent, and even of medicines. Finally, about a year after, when he went home to Scotland on furlough, the city honoured him with a triumphal procession. Banners waved, musical instruments brayed and banged. With native dignity and grandeur the gentry of the place accompanied the man whom they delighted to honour through the streets, out of the gate, and right up to the railway station, where they bade him their best farewell.

As the result of what he had done, the doctor's name and fame spread far and wide through the provinces of Manchuria. Some time afterwards the Rev. Mr. MacNaughtan, going on a prolonged and distant missionary tour, found that right away to the banks of the Yalu River, some 200 miles from Liao-yang, Dr. Westwater's was a name to charm with. Immediately on hearing it mentioned the people would say, "Oh, that was the man who saved Liao-yang."

Hardly less deep was the effect produced by the doctor's character and action upon the Russians in Manchuria. His opinions had weight with the authorities, while he himself became a great personal favourite with all who knew him. Being a Scotchman, Muscovite demonstrativeness often caused him some embarrassment, for a Russian admirer thought nothing of throwing his arms round him and bestowing a hearty kiss. Mr. Whigham tells how he met a Russian engineer, M. Restzoff, who, learning that Mr. Whigham was a Scotchman, said he was glad to make the acquaintance of one who came from

Scotland, for the two greatest men he knew of were both Scotchmen—Dr. Westwater and Sir Walter Scott!

Much water has flowed under the bridges of Manchuria —water often mingled with blood—since the days of the Boxer rising. But the events of more recent years have only added to Dr. Westwater's reputation, and proved once more how much can be done in the interests of humanity and Christianity, amid all "the tumult and the shouting" and the unbridled savagery of war, by a brave, strong man who has devoted his life to the service of his fellow-creatures as a medical missionary.

When the tremendous struggle began between Japan and Russia, Dr. Westwater and his colleague, Mr. Mac Naughtan, together with their wives, were allowed to remain in Liao-yang. This in itself was a tribute to the Doctor's influence, for it is practically certain that but for him the Russians would have expelled the missionaries from the province with the opening of the war. It was the entire confidence felt in him—sufficiently proved by his being in constant demand at headquarters to prescribe for the officers of the army—that enabled the mission to retain its hold upon the city right through the long period of stress and conflict.

As General Kuropatkin had fixed his headquarters at Liao-yang, every fresh disaster to the Russian forces sent an electric thrill through the whole region of which the city formed the centre. And as the opposing armies drew nearer and nearer, the Russians constantly retreating and the Japanese pressing on, the surrounding population began to flock into Liao-yang by tens of thousands. At this stage the doctor obtained General Kuropatkin's permission to open a refuge for these poor homeless creatures, and soon he had four thousand of them, all heathen, under his immediate care.

Meanwhile the tide of battle rolled nearer and nearer. From Mr. MacNaughtan's lips we have received a vivid account of the scenes which were witnessed by Dr. Westwater and himself from the city walls during that long-drawn week of desperate and Titanic encounter which is known as the battle of Liao-yang. Everything lay before them as in a vast panorama—the great Manchurian plain rolling out its length towards the boundary of the distant low hills, the constant stream of ammunition and commissariat waggons flowing on steadily from the station to the battlefield, the sad stream of wounded men flowing as steadily back, the deadly shells bursting nearer and nearer until at length it became no longer possible to stand in safety on the city walls.

Then, after the days of waiting and watching, followed the days of strenuous action. Men, women, and little children, horribly smashed up, began to be carried into the mission hospital, till not only the wards but all the surrounding sheds were crammed with patients. Meanwhile the doctor had his crowded refuge to think of and provide for and be anxious about, for the shells were falling thick, and five times it was hit, though by a merciful providence on every occasion not a single soul within the walls was so much as scratched.

In his *Empire of the East* Mr. Bennet Burleigh, the veteran *doyen* of military correspondents, describes Dr. Westwater as he found him in the thick of his work at this decisive moment of the war. "Brave as a lion," he writes, "Dr. Westwater went about alone, regardless of shellfire and bullets, succouring the wounded and doing good." And then he goes on to tell in more detail what kind of good the doctor was doing in those awful days: how he sheltered the homeless, fed the starving, performed under all the strain of multiplied duties scores of critical operations, and yet found time to show pity and kindness to the crowds of terrified women and helpless children whom war had cast upon his hands.

"I saw the doctor," he says, "just after he had completed seven amputations, and a score more of cases remained to be dealt with." It adds to the impressiveness of Mr. Bennet Burleigh's picture of a hero at the post of duty in a trying hour when he remarks: "He had no assistant—his only helpers a few Chinese who served as nurses." We should supplement Mr. Burleigh's statement, however, by mentioning that while Dr. Westwater was ministering to the heathen refugees, Mr. MacNaughtan, by previous arrangement with his colleague, was devoting himself to the service of the native Christians of Liao-yang in their hour of need.

When the Japanese at length entered the city, they paid their tribute, like the Russians before them, to the value of Dr. Westwater's work. It was their fire, of course, that had wrought the havoc among the non-combatants, but this was an inevitable result of the fact that the Russians had made their last stand at the railway station, and no one more regretted the suffering caused to the people of Liao-yang than the victorious general. One of his first acts was to contribute 1000 yen to Dr. Westwater's hospital and the same sum to his refuge, i.e. in English money, £100 to each.

A ROBBER'S POINT OF VIEW

We have shown something of Dr. Westwater's renown among Chinese citizens and English war correspondents, among the warriors of Russia and Japan alike. It is half amusing to learn that he holds a reputation hardly less distinguished among the robbers and bandits of the Manchurian wilds.

These outlaws, the pests of the country in troublous times, have a happy facility of becoming armed marauders or peaceful villagers at will. The advantages of the doctor's "Free Healing Hall" to a man with a broken limb or an unextracted bullet are not unknown to them, and now and then a robber wounded in some skirmish will find his way into the hospital at Liao-yang, representing himself as a poor peasant who has been attacked and wounded by cruel bandits.

Some time ago a Christian colporteur from the city was travelling through the country districts with his pack of Bibles, Testaments, and tracts. He was passing along a road bordered by a field of ripe millet, when in a moment three or four robbers armed with revolvers sprang out from their hiding-place behind the tall stalks. First of all they relieved him of the money made by his sales, then they opened his pack and looked curiously at his books. "Who are you?" one of them asked. "I belong to the Bible Society," he said. "What is that?" "It is a society of Christians," the man replied. "Ah! Christians!" they shouted, "the society of the foreign devils"; and with that one of them pointed his revolver at the colporteur's head, fingering the trigger meanwhile in a way that was decidedly nasty.

Just then another of the band suddenly stepped forward and asked, "Do you know Dr. Westwater?" "I know him well," the man answered; "he is a member of the Church to which I belong." On hearing this the robber turned to his companions and said, "Do not touch this fellow. Dr. Westwater is a good man. Twc years ago he took a bullet out of my ribs." Whereupon this robber band handed back to the colporteur not only his pack, but every copper of his money, and bade him go in peace on his way to Liao-yang.

Another experience of a somewhat similar kind befell the doctor's colleague, the Rev. Mr. MacNaughtan himself. About a fortnight before the outbreak of the Russo-Japanese War, Mr. MacNaughtan, who had been itinerating in the province, was riding back to Liao-yang. He was drawing near to a strange village, and there was nothing on the road in front of him but a Chinese cart rumbling slowly along. All at once there shot out from the village in a fan-shaped skirmishing formation a band of about twenty horsemen, all armed with rifles. Some of them galloped furiously to right and left, so as to cut off any possibility of escape, but five came straight down the road towards the carter and the missionary.

They met the carter first. One of them, who was mounted on a tall Russian horse, taken no doubt from a murdered Russian soldier, drew up his steed across the road, compelling the cart to stop, and then drawing a heavy whip, began to lash the unfortunate peasant from head to heel.

Mr. MacNaughtan's heart beat fast, for he knew that at that very time Russian outposts were being nipped off every now and then by bands of desperate bandits. He did not know what might be about to befall him. But he thought it best, trusting in God, to put a brave face on the matter and ride straight on.

When he reached the cart the five robbers were drawn up beside it on the road. One of them held his rifle across his saddle ready for use, and all of them looked at him keenly. That he was a European they saw at once, but the Chinese sheepskin robe he wore showed that he was not a Russian, but a missionary. "Where are you going?" they demanded. "To Liao-yang," he replied. "Then pass on," they said. And without the slightest attempt on the part of any one of them to deprive him of his money or to molest him in any way, he was allowed to continue on his journey.

Talking to the present writer of this incident, Mr. MacNaughtan said that he had no doubt whatever that, though not himself a doctor, he owed his escape to the influence of the Liao-yang medical mission. Even to the savage bandits of Manchuria Dr. Westwater is "a good man." Some of them, as has been said, have passed through his hands, and are grateful to him accordingly. Others have heard of his skill and generosity, and if on no higher grounds, entertain a kindly feeling towards him at least from the lower but still effective motive of that form of gratitude which has been defined as "a lively sense of favours to come."

The materials for the above chapter have been derived partly from the pages of the *Missionary Record* of the United Free Church of Scotland, but chiefly from the personal narrative of the Rev. W. MacNaughtan, M.A., of the Presbyterian Mission in Liao-yang.

AFRICA

CHAPTER VII

"THE HERO OF UGANDA"

The kingdom of Mtesa—The young engineer—Victoria Nyanza—The *Daisy*—A *baraza* at Mtesa's court—The land of blood—"Makay lubare"—A Brobdingnagian coffin—King Mwanga and the martyrs—Murder of Bishop Hannington—A visit from Stanley—Mackay's death—An Easter Sunday in the Cathedral of Uganda.

IN days when the British flag flies proudly over the Commissioner's residence in what is now known as the Uganda Protectorate in the equatorial regions of East Central Africa, and railway trains pass regularly to and fro through the wild regions that lie between the town of Mombasa on the coast and Kavirondo Bay on the eastern shores of the Victoria Nyanza, the grandest of all African lakes, most of the mystery and romance which once hung about the kingdom of Uganda may be said to have disappeared. Less than fifty years ago the case was very different. One or two bold travellers, pushing on towards the sources of the Nile, had heard from Arab traders, not less bold, of the existence of an ancient, powerful, and half-civilized kingdom lying directly under the equator, and stretching along the coasts of a great inland sea. But these at the best were only hearsay tales, and if the thrilling romance of *King Solomon's Mines*, dear to the hearts of boys, had been in print half a century ago, the wonderful regions discovered by Allan Quatermain and his companions would have had as much reality to English readers as the dominions of King Mtesa.

But in 1862 Captain Speke reached Uganda, the first of all white men to enter the country; and in 1875 there came an explorer greater still—Henry M. Stanley. Stanley was much impressed by what he saw of Mtesa and his kingdom, and was especially struck with the great possibilities for the future of Christian missions in Africa that seemed to be opened up by the existence in the very heart of the continent of such a country as Uganda, ruled by a monarch so enlightened. On his return to England he wrote a historic letter to a great London newspaper, describing his visit to Uganda, and challenging the Christian Churches of Britain to send missionaries to that land. It was this letter that led the Church Missionary Society, shortly afterwards, to undertake that work in Uganda with which the name of Alexander Mackay will always be associated.

Mackay was a young Scotchman, the son of a Presbyterian minister in Aberdeenshire, who at an early age had made up his mind to devote himself to the service of Christ in the foreign field, and had conceived the original idea of becoming what he called an "engineer missionary." From the first he saw, as most missionary societies have now come to see, that Christianity and modern civilization should go hand in hand, and that mechanical work is as legitimate an aid to missions as medical science. He had a natural bent towards engineering, and after studying it theoretically for three years at Edinburgh University, went to Germany and spent some time there as a draughtsman and constructor. So marked were his constructive talents that one of his employers offered him a partnership in a large engineering concern; but what would have seemed a tempting opportunity to most young men was no temptation to him. Already his heart was in the mission field. When he was twenty-four years of age, and hard at work in Berlin, he wrote in his diary on the first anniversary of Dr. Livingstone's death: "This day last year Livingstone died—a Scotchman and a Christian, loving God and his neighbour in the heart of Africa. 'Go thou and do likewise.'" It was in the year following that Stanley returned from Uganda and wrote the celebrated letter already referred to; and among the first to respond personally to the explorer's challenge was the young Scotch engineer who had drunk so deeply of Livingstone's spirit, and whom Stanley himself described fourteen years later, when he had seen with his own eyes the kind of work that Mackay had done in the heart of Africa, as "the modern Livingstone."

According to Stanley it was the practical Christian teacher who was wanted in the Dark Continent—the man who, sailor-like, could turn his hand to anything. "Such a one," he wrote, "if he can be found, would become the saviour of Africa." Mackay's practical teaching began long before he set foot in Uganda, for as soon as he reached the East African coast he set to work to cut a good road to Mpwapwa, 230 miles inland. It was a huge task for one white man to undertake in the teeth of countless natural difficulties, and in spite of frequent sickness and dangers from wild beasts and savage men. But in the words of the old Scotch proverb, the young engineer "set a stout heart to a stey brae"—fording swamps and climbing hills, bridging rivers and cleaving his way through forests. It was not till two years after he had landed in Africa that he arrived at Kagei on the south of the Victoria Nyanza, and caught his first glimpse of the great lake in the neighbourhood of which the remainder of his life was to be spent. Two of the missionaries for Uganda, Lieutenant Smith and Mr. O'Neill, had been murdered shortly before by a neighbouring king; others had succumbed to the climate one by one; and meantime he was left alone to hold aloft in this vast region the flag of Christianity and civilization.

His first business was to get across the lake, for Kagei is at the south end, while Uganda lies along the north-western shores. In size the Victoria Nyanza is about equal to Ireland, and the only way of crossing this inland sea was by means of a sailing boat called the *Daisy*, which had been brought up from the coast in sections by Lieutenant Smith, but in which not a single sound plank now remained, thanks to the burning rays of the sun, the teeth of hippopotami, and the ravages of armies of white ants. Mackay had to begin without delay those mechanical labours by which he was to produce so deep an impression on the native mind, and which by and by made his name famous all round the shores of the Victoria Nyanza Day by day he toiled single-handed on the beach with crowds of natives all around, willing to help so far as they could, but sometimes doing more to hinder, watching and wondering until, as they saw his turning-lathe at work, or beautiful candles growing under his fingers out of the fat of an ox, or a complete steam-engine out of a heterogeneous collection of bars and rods and bolts and screws, they began to whisper to one another that the white man came from heaven.

But before his boat-building was completed, Mackay impressed the natives in another way by paying a visit to King Lkonge, of the island of Ukerewe, by whose warriors the two missionaries had been murdered a short time before. The friendly people of Kagei entreated him not to go to Ukerewe, assuring him that by doing so he would only be putting his head into the lion's jaws. But he went, alone and unarmed, and got Lkonge to promise that he would allow the missionaries to come and teach his subjects; and then after a nine days' absence returned to Kagei, where he was received almost as one who had come back from the dead.

At length the *Daisy* was ready, and Mackay had now to undertake the duty of navigating her across the unknown waters. Even to an experienced sailor like the murdered Lieutenant Smith the task would not have been an easy one, for like the Sea of Galilee, the Victoria Nyanza is a lake of storms, while countless rocks and islets stud the broad expanse on every hand. And Mackay was not only no sailor, he had not the slightest acquaintance with the art of handling a sailing boat. Still there was nothing for it but to launch out into the deep with a native crew which knew even less about boats than he did himself. It was a terrible voyage. Soon after leaving Kagei a great storm came down and raged upon the lake for two days, during which the *Daisy* was driven helplessly before the fury of wind and waves, until she was hurled at last a mere wreck upon the western coast. The boat-builder's task had to be resumed once more; and the *Daisy* was repaired, as Mackay himself puts it, "much as one would make a pair of shoes out of a pair of long boots. Cutting eight feet out of the middle of her, we brought stem and stern together, patching up all broken parts in these with the wood of the middle portion; and after eight weeks' hard labour, we launched her once more on the Victoria Nyanza."

It was not till November, 1878, two and a half years after leaving England, that Ntebe, the port of Uganda, was sighted at last; and five days afterwards Mackay entered Rubaga, the capital of the land which had so long been the goal of all his hopes and efforts. On the earliest day on which there was a *baraza* or levee at Mtesa's court, he received a summons to attend. It was a striking succession of scenes that met his quietly observant eye as he passed along the magnificently wide road that led to the royal palace of this Central African city. In his *Two Kings of Uganda* Mr. Ashe, Mackay's colleague at a later period, gives a graphic account of one of Mtesa's levees, when, amidst the rolling tattoos of deep-toned drums and the blare of trumpets, lords and chieftains from far and near, villainous but smiling Arabs, runaway Egyptian soldiers from the Soudan, adventurers from the East Coast and Madagascar, mountebanks, minstrels, dancers, and dwarfs all gathered into the courtyard of the Kabaka, which was the native title of the king.

Mackay's presentation passed off very well, and it was

not long till his great skill in all kinds of arts and crafts, and especially in ironwork, made him an object of wonder to the whole country and a special favourite with the king. But he never allowed himself to forget that, important as practical work was, there was something which was infinitely higher, and that all the influence which he gained by his mechanical ingenuity must be turned to the service of the Gospel he had come to Uganda to proclaim. So while during the rest of the week he practised the arts of civilization and imparted them to others, when Sunday came he regularly presented himself at the court, and read and expounded the New Testament to a listening crowd in the presence of the king. At first Mtesa appeared to be in sympathy with his teaching, and to the ardent young missionary it almost seemed as if the whole nation of Uganda might be born in a day. It was not long, however, till adverse influences began to work. The Arab traders bitterly disliked Mackay, for they were well aware that all his influence went to undermine their very lucrative slave trade. There were some Roman Catholic priests, too, who had followed him to Uganda after he had opened up the way, and these men set themselves to prejudice both king and people against him as far as they could. But worst of all, Mtesa turned out to be a hearer of the type of that Felix to whom St. Paul preached. Up to a certain point he listened to Mackay willingly enough, but he did not like the missionary to get into close grips with his conscience. There was much that was good and amiable about Mtesa, and to the end he protected Mackay from all his enemies. But his whole previous life had been a training in cruelty, brutality, and lust; and though his mind was convinced of the truth of the Christian Gospel, its moral demands were too much for his taste, and he remained a heathen in heart.

And so there came a time when Mackay discovered to his horror that while for more than two years the king had been listening to him with apparent interest, he had been permitting almost unimaginable cruelties to be practised just as before. In particular, every now and then he gave orders for a *kiwendo*, i.e. a great massacre of human victims, in one of which as many as 2,000 persons were put to death in a single day. In anticipation of these great sacrifices, gangs of executioners prowled about the land by night, pouncing upon innocent and helpless people and marching them off to the capital; and by and by Mackay came to know that the deep roll of drums which sometimes wakened him in the dead of night was nothing else than the signal that a fresh batch of victims had been brought in. When the day of the *kiwendo* arrived, these wretched creatures were put to death by burning. But before being cast alive into the flames many had their eyes put out, their noses and ears cut off, or the sinews of their arms and thighs torn out and roasted before their faces.

Against these horrible deeds Mackay protested with all his strength, but only offended the king, who now declined to see him at the court, and no longer as at first supplied him with food, so that he and the two other missionaries by whom he had been joined were sometimes reduced to actual starvation. From time to time, however, the royal favour was regained in some measure by a fresh demonstration of the white man's mechanical power. Once in a time of great drought, when water was not to be had in the capital, Mackay sank a deep well—a thing which had never before been seen in Uganda, and fitted it with a pump—a thing more wonderful still. And when the people saw the copious stream of water ascending twenty feet high, and flowing on as long as any one worked the pump handle, their astonishment knew no bounds, and they cried, *Makay lubare* ("Mackay is the great spirit") again and again. But their benefactor did not trade on their ignorance. He told them that the pump was only a kind of elephant's trunk made of copper, or that it was like the tubes they used for sucking beer out of their beer jars, only much bigger and with a tongue of iron to suck up the water. "I am no great spirit," he assured them. "There is only one Great Spirit, that is God; and I am only a man like yourselves."

Another of Mackay's tasks at this time was imposed on him by the death of Mtesa's mother, and consisted in the manufacture of what the king considered a fitting receptacle for the corpse of so august a personage. It was a triple series of coffins—an inner one of wood, a middle one of copper, and an outer one of wood covered with cloth. Everything had to be made as large as possible, and to fulfil the office of undertaker on this Brobdingnagian scale the handy missionary had to toil incessantly for thirty days, and latterly all through the night as well. The outer coffin was made of 100 boards nailed together, with strong ribs like the sides of a schooner, and was so enormous that it looked like a house rather than a coffin, and required the assistance of a whole army of men that it might be lowered safely into the grave, which, again, was a huge pit twenty feet long, fifteen feet broad, and about thirty feet deep.

At last Mtesa died, worn out prematurely by his vices, and was succeeded by his son Mwanga, a youth of about seventeen, who inherited his father's worst qualities, but none of his good ones. Then began a time of fiery trial for the mission. Mackay and his companions were daily threatened with death, and death was made the penalty of listening to their teaching or even of reading the Bible in secret. Many of Mackay's pupils and converts were tortured and burnt to death; but in Uganda as elsewhere the old saying came true that "the blood of the martyrs is the seed of the Church." Inquirers became far more numerous than ever; men stole into the houses of the missionaries by night and begged to be baptized; and there were cases where bolder ones went openly to the court and proclaimed that they were Christians, though they knew that their confession would immediately be followed by a cruel death. Sir H. M. Stanley said of this martyr Church of Uganda that he took it to be "a more substantial evidence of the work of Mackay than any number of imposing structures clustered together and called a mission station would be." Certain it is that it was by the tearful sowing of Mackay and his companions in those gloomy days that there was brought about that time of plentiful and joyful reaping which came in Uganda by and by.

And now we come to the culminating tragedy in this story of tyranny and bloodshed, and the moment when the faith and courage of the missionaries were most severely tested. They knew that Mr. Hannington had been consecrated Bishop of East Equatorial Africa and was on his way to Uganda from the coast. And they had heard with much concern that, instead of following the customary route to the south end of the lake, he was marching through the Masai country on the east towards the district of Usoga at the northern extremity of the Victoria Nyanza, with the intention of entering Uganda from that quarter. The ground of their concern lay in the fact that the people of Uganda looked upon Usoga as their private "back door," through which no strangers, and especially no white men, should be permitted to approach. There was an old prophecy among them that their country was to be conquered by a people coming from the east, and when word was brought that white men with a large caravan of followers had made their appearance in Usoga, Mwanga and his councillors grew excited and alarmed. Mackay guessed at once who the advancing travellers would be, and did everything he could to reassure the king as to Hannington's purpose in coming to his country. But in spite of all his efforts, a band of soldiers was secretly dispatched to intercept and massacre the Bishop and his followers; and soon the news spread throughout all Uganda that Mwanga's instructions had been literally fulfilled. The murder of the Bishop seemed to whet the tyrant's appetite for Christian blood, and a general persecution followed in which the very flower of the native converts were slain, while the lives of the missionaries themselves constantly hung by a single thread—the king being kept from ordering their instant execution only by the powerful influence of his Katikoro or Prime Minister, who urged him to remember all that Mackay had done for his father in the past.

At length Mr. Ashe, Mackay's only remaining companion, got permission to return to England, while Mackay himself was allowed to withdraw to the south end of the lake. Much as he needed a rest, he could not be persuaded to turn his back on Africa at this critical juncture. Nor did he cross the lake through any personal fears, but only because he was convinced that it might be best for the native Christians that his presence should be removed for a time. He went accordingly to the district of Usambiro, south of the lake, and immediately started mission work there, devoting himself at the same time to the task of translating and printing portions of Scripture for the Uganda people, so that even in his absence the Divine word might continue to win its way in many hearts.

It was whilst he was at Usambiro that Stanley and he first met. The distinguished explorer was then on his way back to the coast after his relief of Emin Pasha, and to him and his companions it was a welcome relief, as several of them have testified—an oasis in the desert of African travel,—to come in the midst of their long and weary march upon Mackay's mission station at Usambiro. In his book, *In Darkest Africa* (vol. II, pp. 388–389), Stanley himself gives a graphic description of the meeting, and thus records his impressions of the young Scotch missionary and the work in which they found him quietly and steadily engaged:—

"Talking thus, we entered the circle of tall poles within which the mission station was built. There were signs of labour and constant, unwearying patience, sweating under a hot sun, a steadfast determination to do something to keep the mind employed, and never let idleness find them with folded hands brooding over the unloveliness, lest despair might seize them and cause them to avail themselves of the speediest means of ending their misery. There was a big, solid workshop in the yard, filled with machinery and tools, a launch's boiler was being prepared by the blacksmiths, a big canoe was outside repairing; there were sawpits and large logs of hard timber, there were great stacks of palisade poles, in a corner of an outer yard was a cattle-fold and a goat-pen, fowls by the score pecked at microscopic grains, and out of the European quarter there trooped a number of little boys and big boys looking uncommonly sleek and happy, and quiet labourers came up to bid us, with hats off, 'Good morning!'

* * * * *

"A clever writer lately wrote a book about a man who spent much time in Africa, which from beginning to end is a long-drawn wail. It would have cured both writer and hero of all moping to have seen the manner of Mackay's life. He has no time to fret and groan and weep; and God knows, if ever man had reason to think of 'graves and worms and oblivion,' and to be doleful and lonely and sad, Mackay had, when, after murdering his Bishop, and burning his pupils, and strangling his converts, and clubbing to death his dark friends, Mwanga turned his eye of death on him. And yet the little man met it with calm blue eyes that never winked. To see one man of this kind working day after day for twelve years bravely, and without a syllable of complaint or a moan amid the 'wildernesses,' and to hear him lead his little flock to show forth God's loving-kindness in the morning and His faithfulness every night, is worth going a long journey for the moral courage and contentment that one derives from it."

Stanley spent twenty days at Usambiro, enjoying to the full the society and hospitality of his missionary friend. On the day that the expedition left Mackay walked with the travellers for some distance, but bade them good-bye at last, and stood on the path waving his hat till they passed out of sight. One of Stanley's officers wrote afterwards, "That lonely figure standing on the brow of the hill, waving farewell to us, will ever remain vividly in my mind."

The end of this heroic life came not long after. Mackay was struck down in the midst of his labours by a sharp attack of malarial fever, which he had not the strength to resist, and after some days of delirium he passed quietly away. He has been called "The Hero of Uganda," and the record of his life shows that he would be worthy of the name, even though no great apparent fruitage had come from all his toils and trials. But the events that have followed since his death help us to a clearer estimate of the richness of the seeds he sowed, often in manifold pain and sorrow, in those first days of Christianity on the shores of the Victoria Nyanza. The Rev. J. S. Moffat, son of the celebrated Dr. Moffat and brother-in-law of Dr. Livingstone, writing in August, 1904, in the *Aurora*, the journal of the Livingstonia

Presbyterian Mission on the west of Lake Nyasa, gives a vivid description of a recent visit to Uganda, and thus pictures the scene he witnessed on Easter Sunday in the Cathedral Church at Namirembe :—

"From where I sat I could see at least three thousand faces. I was told that there was still a crowd outside—of those who could not find room: and there was a separate and simultaneous service being conducted in an adjacent building, at which at least five hundred younger people were assembled. In the cathedral we joined in the stately service of the Anglican Church, never so stately and impressive as when it is rendered in noble simplicity, free from the adventitious accompaniment and the vicarious performance of a highly artistic choir.

"There was something more real and solemn than this in the vast murmur, almost a thunder-roll, of thousands of responding voices, the voices of men and women who had been born in the most degraded and darkest heathenism, the people that sat in darkness but had seen a great light; the Easter sun shining upon the stone that had been rolled away, and upon the open grave."

NOTE.—The chief authorities for Mackay's life are *Mackay of Uganda* and *The Story of Mackay of Uganda*, both written by his sister, and published by Hodder and Stoughton; *Two Kings of Uganda*, by Rev. R. P. Ashe, M.A. (Sampson, Low, Marston, and Co.).

CHAPTER VIII

THE LION-HEARTED BISHOP

"Mad Jim"—An ideal pioneer—A novel way of landing in Africa—"Teek, teek, teek"—Encounter with lions—Turned back from the goal—Bishop of East Equatorial Africa—The new route to Uganda—Through Masailand—The El Moran—Greasy bed-fellows—The forbidden land—Martyrdom.

THERE is no chapter in the story of modern missions which has more of the romantic element about it than that which tells how the Kingdom of Uganda, within less than a generation, was turned from a land of heathen darkness and cruelty to one in which on the Lord's Day such scenes of devout Christian worship are to be witnessed in church and cathedral as are described on a preceding page in the language of the Rev. Mr. Moffat. We have spoken of Alexander Mackay as the hero of Uganda; and undoubtedly it was he more than any other who sowed in that land the seed which has been reaped so plentifully since. But there is another name which the Church of Uganda must ever cherish side by side with Mackay's—the name of that lion-hearted man, Bishop Hannington, who literally laid down his life for her sake. It is true that Hannington never saw Uganda. And yet during his brief missionary career it was for Uganda most of all that he prayed and toiled and suffered, and it was for Uganda, too, that he died at last a martyr's death. When the soldiers of the cruel Mwanga were about to thrust their spears into his body as he stood on the very threshold of the land he had sought so long, he bade them tell their king "that he was about to die for Uganda, and that he had purchased the road to Uganda with his life."

James Hannington was the very ideal of a pioneer missionary. Full of physical vitality and animal spirits, and absolutely devoid of fear, he spent his boyhood in all kinds of adventures by land and water, which sometimes developed into schoolboy scrapes of the kind that Mr. Kipling describes so vividly in *Stalky & Co.* When only twelve, he had the thumb of his left hand blown off by some damp gunpowder squibs or "blue devils," which he had manufactured with a view to taking a wasp's nest. And in after years, when a young curate, he often alarmed the parishioners by his reckless feats as a climber and egg-hunter on the Devonshire cliffs.

But in the heart of "Mad Jim," as he had been called at school, there grew up a great love for Christ, and a desire to serve Him in the ministry of the Church. And when he took Holy Orders, after studying at Oxford, it proved that his adventurous spirit, his athletic habits, and his frank outspoken manliness gave him a power over many minds which the ordinary clergyman mostly fails to reach. By and by the stirrings of the heart began to urge him forth to a larger and more difficult field than he could find at home. In particular, when word came to England of the murder of Lieutenant Smith and Mr. O'Neill on the Victoria Nyanza, he felt the impulse of the brave soldier to step into the gap where a comrade has fallen. And when the Church Missionary Society decided to send a fresh party to Uganda to reinforce Mackay, who was holding the ground with a single companion in the face of infinite difficulties and discouragements, Hannington was one of the first to volunteer. He was most happily settled by this time as incumbent of St. George's Chapel, Hurstpierpoint, the home of his boyhood and youth, and had besides a wife and young children to whom he was

First Landing in Africa

From a sketch by Bishop Hannington

passionately attached. But the call he heard was one to which he could give no denial. For Christ and for Africa he felt that he must be willing to suffer the loss of all things.

Hannington was appointed leader of the new party, which consisted of six men; and his instructions were to endeavour to reach Uganda from Zanzibar by what was then the ordinary route, viz., to the south end of the

Victoria Nyanza, and thereafter by boat across the Lake to Rubaga, King Mtesa's capital. His first landing in Africa was thoroughly like himself. The thirty miles of channel between Zanzibar and the mainland was crossed in a filthy Arab dhow, but the water was so shallow that the vessel could not get within half a mile of the shore. A dug-out canoe put off to their assistance, in which the rest of the passengers were conveyed to land two or three at a time. But as the sea was rough the waves broke constantly over the canoe, nearly filling it with water. Hannington said "that he preferred a regular bathe to a foot-bath with his boots on. So he stripped off his clothes, put them into a bag which he carried on his head, and disregarding the sharks, he waded and stumbled and swam over the half-mile of rough coral and through the breakers which lay between the vessel and the beach. So he landed on the coast of Africa in a manner quite characteristic."

When Hannington went up for his examination before being ordained, he did not make a very brilliant appearance, and the Bishop, after looking him all over, said, "You've got fine legs, I see: mind that you run about your parish." His parish now was East Central Africa; and it was well that he had good legs. Practically the whole of his life as a missionary was spent in journeying up and down this vast region. But to a man of his temperament, though the motive of carrying the Gospel to the heart of the African continent was the central one, exploration and adventure were very welcome in themselves, and he entered into his new experiences with much of the zest of his boyish days. Here is a description written to his nephews and nieces, and accompanied by one of those droll sketches with which he often embellished his letters to familiar friends:—

"Fancy a set of hideous savages regarding your uncle as a strange, outlandish creature, frightful to behold! 'Are those your feet, white man?' 'No, gentlemen, they

THE BISHOP AND THE MUTINOUS BOATMAN

From a sketch by Bishop Hannington

are not. They are my sandals.' 'But, do they grow to your feet?' 'No, gentlemen, they do not; I will show you.' So I would unlace a boot. A roar of astonishment followed when they saw my blue sock, as they thought my feet must be blue and toeless. I pulled off the sock, and they were dumbfounded at the sight of my white, five-toed foot. They used to think that only my face and hands were white, and the rest of me black like themselves. My watch, too, was an unfailing attraction. 'There is a man in it.' 'It is *Lubari*; it is witchcraft,' they would cry. 'He talks; he says, Teek, teek, teek.' My nose they they would compare with a spear, it struck them as so sharp and thin as compared with their own. Often one would give my hair a smart pull to try whether it were a wig and would come off."

There were times when the experiences of the travellers were more dangerous than amusing, for there were murderous robbers in some of the forests, who were ever on the watch to pounce upon unwary strangers, and there were deep pits, cunningly covered over with twigs and grass, and with upright spears at the bottom, which were used by the natives as traps for the larger kinds of game. To stumble into one of these means almost certainly a horrible death. Hannington himself fell into one, but fortunately in this case the spears were wanting; and he was not dangerously hurt, though much shaken and bruised.

It was fitting that this lion-hearted missionary should have more than one exciting encounter with lions. The most thrilling of all took place one day when he had gone out to shoot, accompanied by a single boy. Seeing a small animal moving through the long grass in front, he fired, and the creature rolled over quite dead. On coming up to it he discovered that it was nothing less than a lion's whelp. Immediately the boy shouted, "Run, master, run!" and took to his heels as hard as he could. His terror was not premature, for the next moment, with terrific roars, a large lion and lioness came bounding towards Hannington out of the jungle. His gun was empty, he had no time to reload; but though his natural impulse was to run, he felt at once that this would be fatal. So he stood his ground, and when the lions came near growling and lashing their tails and glaring at this intruder, he only glared back at them with steady eyes.

A VISIT FROM A HIPPOPOTAMUS

From a sketch by Bishop Hannington

This unflinching courage completely subdued them, and as they stood staring fiercely at him, he gradually retreated backwards for a hundred yards or so, facing them all the while, and then turned and quietly walked away. Most men, however brave, would have been content with this victory. But Hannington was not content; for he now determined to go back and secure the young lion's skin if possible. As he drew near again he saw that the lion and its mate were walking round and round the dead body of their whelp, licking it, and turning it over, and trying to restore it to life. Throwing his arms into the air and yelling as loud as he could, he rushed forward; and the fierce beasts, which evidently had never met such a person as this before, fairly turned tail and leaped away into the bush. Whereupon Hannington seized his prize, and by and by marched into camp carrying it triumphantly on his shoulders.

The Victoria Nyanza was reached about Christmas, 1882, after a weary journey of several months, marked not only by dangers from lions, leopards, rhinos, and buffaloes, but by constant worries and anxieties due to the fact that the expedition was very badly provided with supplies. At first it seemed to Hannington that his journey was almost at an end, for only the great sheet of water now separated him from Uganda. But, like Mackay before him, he soon found that his worst troubles were yet to come. In the meantime they had no means of crossing, and while Hannington toiled to make arrangements he took a violent attack of malarial fever, and was quickly reduced to such terrible weakness that his companions agreed that his only chance of saving his life lay in returning to England immediately. And so when almost within sight of his goal he had to turn back, and allow himself to be carried in a hammock all the dreary way back to Zanzibar. Catching a mail steamer, he got safely home to England, and was received again into his beloved circle at Hurstpierpoint "almost," as his biographer Mr. Dawson puts it, "as one alive from the dead."

THE TASK RESUMED

At first it seemed certain that he would never see Africa again; but gradually his strength returned, and with it a keen desire to resume the task he had undertaken. Meantime the directors of the Church Missionary Society, who had long been anxious to secure a Bishop to take the oversight of all the churches they had planted in East Central Africa, singled him out as pre-eminently qualified for the position, and the Archbishop of Canterbury cordially agreed to consecrate him. In the summer of 1884, accordingly, he became Bishop of East Equatorial Africa, a diocese which embraced not Uganda only, but the immense region which lies between the Victoria Nyanza and the coast. Uganda, however, was still his chief concern, and his failure to reach it on the first attempt made him all the more determined to visit it now without delay, and to endeavour to bring some comfort to its persecuted Christians and some help to the brave Mackay, who still held the fort for Christ and the Church in that unhappy land in which the debased and cruel Mwanga was now king.

Having set things in order at the stations near the coast, and paid a flying visit to Mount Kilimanjaro for the purpose of planting the banner of the cross upon its very slopes, the Bishop therefore began at once to make preparations for his second and last journey towards Uganda. And now he came to what proved to be a fateful decision. Hitherto the missionaries had started from Zanzibar and made for the south end of the lake, thereafter crossing the Victoria Nyanza in boats. But Hannington knew by painful experience the difficulties of that route—its undue length, its exasperating delays, the deadly influences of its fever-haunted swamps. He conceived the idea of a new line of march which, starting not from Zanzibar but from Mombasa, about 150 miles nearer the Equator, should aim not at the south of the lake but at the north. For one thing, this route would be considerably shorter. Moreover, as his brief visit to Kilimanjaro had shown, instead of passing through a low-lying country, it would lead to a large extent over healthy uplands where travelling would be safe for Europeans. The one great difficulty he thought of, a difficulty which until lately had seemed insurmountable, was the fact that he would be obliged to traverse the country of the Masai, whose very name was a word of terror for hundreds of miles around. But not long before, that intrepid young Scotchman, Mr. Joseph Thomson, had explored the Masai country without coming to any harm; and a close study of his fascinating book, *Through Masai Land*, had set the Bishop thinking. If an explorer could make his way among the Masai, why not a Christian missionary? Anyhow, he meant to try, for he was convinced that if this route was at all practicable, the choice of it in the future would mean to the Society an immense saving of time and money, as well as of precious lives.

Unfortunately there was one element in the case which escaped all Hannington's calculations, and brought about the tragedy of which we have to tell. He did not know that the kings of Uganda regarded the country of Usoga, to the north of the lake, through which he would have to pass, as their "back door," by which no white man must be allowed to enter. Nor was he aware that that very journey of Joseph Thomson's, from which he was

Bishop Hannington's Encounter with an Elephant and a Rhinoceros drawing encouragement, had caused a great flutter at the court of Mtesa, and that it was well for that bold traveller that he had turned back after merely touching the lake at its north-eastern extremity, without attempting to advance farther. No blame, however, can be ascribed to the Bishop for his ignorance, nor can he be accused of acting rashly. His plans were made with the approval of both the Sultan of Zanzibar and Sir John Kirk, the British Consul, with the latter of whom he had frequent consultations before starting on his ill-fated journey.

In the meantime something like his old strength and vigour had returned, as may be judged from the fact that, on a preliminary tramp up country in connexion with some of his episcopal duties, he marched back to the coast, a distance of 120 miles, in exactly three days and half an hour—forty miles a day on an average—a feat which is perhaps unexampled in the annals of African travel.

It was in July, 1885, that he finally set off from Mombasa at the head of a caravan 200 strong. He knew that he must be prepared to face many dangers. "Starvation," he wrote, "desertion, treachery, and a few other nightmares and furies hover over our heads in ghastly forms." But nothing disturbed the flow of his spirits. His biographer gives us this glimpse of the Bishop on the march: "All the way during that march to Taita his letters reveal him to us, till we seem to see him as he strides ahead with that springy step of his. Arms swinging, eyes ever on the alert to notice anything new or remarkable, now a snatch of song, again a shout of encouragement, a leap upon some rare flower or insect—the very life and soul of his company, while ever and anon his emphatic voice would be raised in the notes of some old familiar tune, and the wilderness would ring to the sound of a Christian hymn—

> "Peace, perfect peace, the future all unknown;
> Jesus we know, and He is on the throne."

By and by his correspondence ceases, as he vanishes into a region which knows not the post office even in its most primitive forms. Fortunately, however, his little pocket-diary was recovered from one of the band that murdered him, and much additional light has been shed upon that last journey by Mr. Jones, a newly ordained native clerygyman whom he had taken with him as his companion.

The new route proved to be less easy than Hannington had hoped, and the caravan, besides having to fight its way through obstinate jungles, had a good deal of trouble with unfriendly natives, even before reaching the land of the much-dreaded Masai—the scourges at that time of East Central Africa. The Masai are not negroes, or members of the great Bantu family by which the greater part of the African continent is inhabited, but belong to what ethnologists call the Hamitic race, occupying a distinctly higher position in the scale of humanity. Up to the age of thirty, Mr. Joseph Thomson tells us, every young Masai is a warrior, and these warriors, or El Moran as they are called, live in huge kraals or military barracks large enough to accommodate 2000 of them at a time, from which they issue periodically on murdering

A Mock Duel between Two Masai Warriors

and marauding expeditions. The arrogance and insolence of the warrior class is unbounded, while any attempt at resenting it is met at once by the uplifting of a forest of their great broad-bladed spears.

With these Masai Bishop Hannington had a trying time. It was quite impossible to keep the young warriors out of his tent, and they came crowding in at their pleasure demanding *hongo*, which is the name for an enforced present, and making themselves free with everything. His chair, his bed, his wash-tub, his biscuit-boxes were all covered with dirty, sprawling figures, and he himself was subjected to impertinences of every kind. They stroked his hair, pulled his beard, felt his cheeks, and tried on his clothes; and not only fingered all his personal belongings, but spat upon them, that being the Masai token of appreciation. Again and again destruction seemed to be hanging over the camp by a single thread, for the El Moran like nothing better than an excuse for slaughter, and if any one had lost his temper for a moment, it might have been the signal for a wholesale massacre. But at this time the Bishop and his men were mercifully preserved. He notes in his diary, "I strove in prayer; and each time trouble seemed to be averted." And it would appear that even those fierce people felt the power of Hannington's brotherliness. They were by no means agreeable company, with their spitting habits, and the grease and red earth with which they daubed their bodies and so smeared everything they touched. But once when three of them had come with an ox for sale, Hannington invited them to stay with him all night, as it was getting late and their kraal was far off; and, rather to his surprise, they consented quite gratefully. So the Bishop and the three warriors lay down side by side on the floor of the little tent, and though the Masai slept with their spears beside them, he neither showed nor felt the slightest fear. He writes, "They packed themselves away like sardines in a box, and I covered them over first with a leopard's skin, then with a grass mat, and finally a waterproof sheet. They fell almost instantly into a most gentle sleep. I followed their example and, with one exception, I did not wake up until time to start. Wherever we meet we are to be brothers."

Soon after passing through the Masai country the travellers came to Kavirondo, a region which no white man but Mr. Joseph Thomson had ever visited, while even he had not attempted to go farther. Between them and Uganda nothing now lay but the forbidden land of Usoga. At this stage, owing to the uncertainty of the route, Hannington decided to leave Mr. Jones with the bulk of the caravan encamped in Kavirondo, and to push on himself towards Uganda with fifty of his men.

News travels swiftly even in Africa, and the cruel Mwanga was by this time perfectly aware of the white man's advance, and, as we learn from Mackay, was greatly concerned about it. Mackay did all he could to reassure the king and his advisers, but without effect. Mwanga decided that this daring stranger must die, and sent orders to Lubwa, an Usoga chief, who was his puppet in the matter, to have him and his followers arrested. For fully a week they were kept in close confinement, until a band of Mwanga's soldiers arrived with secret orders to put them all to death.

BISHOP HANNINGTON A PRISONER SHORTLY BEFORE HIS MARTYRDOM

He was kept in a fair-sized hut with about twenty men around him. The place was very dirty, and quite dark but for the firelight.

The Bishop was led through the forest to a place some miles distant from the scene of his imprisonment, and there he found his men before him, stripped naked and bound with thongs. His own clothing was then roughly torn off; and he saw that the end was near. Although weak with fever and greatly reduced by his trying imprisonment, his courage never failed him in that awful hour. He gave his murderers that message to their king to which we referred at the beginning of this chapter; and then kneeling down, he committed his soul to God. A moment after the fierce soldiers rushed upon their victims with their stabbing spears. Two of them, who had been told off for the purpose and were stationed one on either side of Hannington, plunged their weapons into his heart, while all around him the ground was covered with his dead and dying men.

The diary which he kept during his imprisonment is exceedingly touching, especially the entries of the last two days. It was on a Thursday that he died, and on Wednesday we find him writing: "A terrible night, first with noisy drunken guard, and secondly with vermin, which have found out my tent and swarm. I don't think I got one sound hour's sleep, and woke with fever fast developing. O Lord, do have mercy upon me and release me. I am quite broken down and brought low. Comforted by reading Psalm XXVII." The last entry of all is very brief. It must have been written just before the soldiers came to lead him out to die.

"*Oct. 29th, Thursday* (Eighth day's prison).—I can hear no news, but was held up by Psalm XXX, which came with great power. A hyena howled near me last night, smelling a sick man, but I hope it is not to have me yet."

Our knowledge of the final scenes comes partly from the testimony of three or four of Hannington's men, whose lives were spared on condition that they would show the murderers how to open his boxes, partly from the evidence of some of the soldiers themselves, who subsequently became members of the Uganda Church, but especially from one of his porters, a young coast Christian, who was with the Bishop to the very last, and was speared by his side and left on the ground for dead. During the night he revived and crawled for miles through the forest, with his bowels protruding from a dreadful wound, till he reached the tent of a native who was a friend of Mackay's, and by whom he was kindly received and tended until his recovery.

So died the lion-hearted Bishop at the comparatively early age of thirty-eight. But "we live in deeds, not years"; and the brave simplicity of his character, together with his martyr death, will keep his name alive as one of the truest of the many missionary heroes of "Darkest Africa."

AUTHORITIES.—*James Hannington* and *Lion-Hearted*, both by Rev. E. C. Dawson, M.A. (London: Seeley and Co.); *Through Masai Land*, by Joseph Thomson London: Sampson Low, Marston Searle, and Rivington.

CHAPTER IX

PIONEERS IN NYASALAND

Up the Zambesi and the Shiré—Lake Nyasa—Dr. Livingstone and Livingstonia—The first pioneers—Gravestones and milestones—The wild Angoni—A raid and a rescue—A great *indaba*—Arab slavers—The Arab war—African Lakes Corporation—Transformation of Central Africa—A dream-city.

THE traveller to Nyasaland who has been carried swiftly to the Far South and round the Cape of Good Hope by one of the great steamers of the Union Castle Line, and has next sailed up the East African coast on a German liner, may find after arriving at the mouth of the Zambesi that the remaining stages of his journey take nearly as long as the ocean voyage of 10,000 miles. First comes a tedious struggle up the Zambesi in a river steamboat which proceeds only by day, since it would be impossible to pilot her through the snags and shallows at night, and sometimes sticks on a sandbank, so that, crocodiles notwithstanding, the black crew has to tumble into the water and try to drag her off. By and by, after entering the Shire, that great northern tributary of the Zambesi which flows out of Lake Nyasa itself, the steamboat is exchanged for a barge propelled by poles. The barge is provided with a tiny deck-house in which the traveller is supposed to spend his nights, but if he is wise he will climb with his pillow on to the house roof, where as he lies he can catch the night breeze and listen drowsily before falling asleep to the lullabies of innumerable frogs, and see the fireflies flitting through the reeds on the river bank and the Southern Cross gleaming before him like the chief jewel of a diadem on "the forehead of the sky." When the Shiré Highlands are reached and the rapids begin, he must betake himself to *terra firma* for an overland journey of a few days via Blantyre, the Central African namesake of Dr. Livingstone's Scottish birthplace, for this whole region of the Zambesi, the Shiré, and Lake Nyasa with its western hinterland, is consecrated more than any other part of the Dark Continent to the memory of the greatest of missionary explorers. Having rounded the rapids, partly by the help of a brand-new railway line and partly in a *machila*, or hammock slung on a bamboo pole and carried by relays of sturdy natives, our traveller arrives at the Upper Shiré, where the river is navigable once more, and soon is again steaming onwards. At last comes a red-letter day in his experience when he reaches Fort Johnston, where his vessel glides out from between the river banks into the broad blue expanse of Lake Nyasa stretching northwards for 350 miles.

It is a slow and sometimes painful progress, this journey to Nyasaland from the coast; and yet how swift and easy and luxurious compared with what it was little more than a generation ago when Dr. Livingstone died! But even more striking than the changes brought about in Central Africa by the introduction of steam and the making of

The Native Method of Carrying Whites in Livingstonia

roads is the transformation wrought by the coming of a Christian civilization. When Livingstone explored the Zambesi and discovered the Shiré River and the magnificent lake by which it is fed, Arab slave-raiders were devastating the whole country by their abominable traffic with its accompaniment of outrage and massacre. Wherever he went he saw skeletons scattered about the bush, villages left without a single inhabitant, corpses floating down the streams in such numbers that he could not keep count of them—showing that the very crocodiles were gorged to satiety with human flesh. To this great-hearted man it seemed that his brother's blood was crying to heaven out of the ground, and he made a passionate appeal to the Christian people of Britain to heal what he described as "the open sore of the world." Not till after his lonely death in the heart of Africa and his burial in Westminster Abbey did his words have their full effect. But the voice of the dead hero touched his countrymen as the voice of the living one had never done. Especially was this the case in Scotland, which claimed Livingstone as her very own. The Established Church of Scotland entered upon its noble work at Blantyre in the Shiré Highlands, while the Free Church (now the United Free Church) founded on the shores of Lake Nyasa that remarkable Livingstonia Mission of which the present chapter is to tell.

It was in the month of July, 1875, that Lieutenant Young, R.N., and a party which included the Rev. Dr. Laws (a qualified medical man), who may be described as the veteran and hero of Nyasaland, together with a carpenter, a blacksmith, an engineer, an agriculturist, and a seaman, found themselves dumped down at the Zambesi mouth after a dangerous voyage from the Cape in a small German schooner called the *Hara*. As part of their equipment they had brought with them a little steamer, the *Ilala*, built in sections, and as soon as they had succeeded in fitting it together, they started on their journey upstream. A toilsome journey it proved, for the *Ilala* had been built for service on the lake rather than the rivers, and was constantly going aground and requiring to be emptied of its cargo, and then hauled off into deeper water. When the Murchison Cataracts were reached, where for sixty miles the Shiré rushes swiftly down from its upper reaches towards the lower levels of the Zambesi by a succession of falls and rapids, their little transport had to be taken to pieces again, and dragged with terrible toil over the long portage to the Upper Shiré, where once again it was rebuilt and relaunched. By that time, however, the journey's end was well in sight. Three or four days of quiet steaming brought them safely at last to the lake of their hopes and dreams. Of the little *Ilala* it might be said not only that she was—

> The first that ever burst
> Into that silent sea,

but that she was the first steam vessel to float on any of the great lakes of Central Africa, the forerunner of the numerous steamers that ply up and down the waters of Lake Nyasa, Lake Tanganyika, Victoria Nyanza, and the other inland seas of the continent.

The first settlement of these pioneers was at Cape Maclear, a beautiful promontory at the south end of the lake, where before long the leadership of the enterprise fell upon Dr. Laws, Lieutentant Young being recalled by the Admiralty to his naval duties, from which he had only obtained temporary leave of absence. From life in Central Africa an element of danger is never quite wanting. Those who have moved through the forests and along the streams can tell many a tale of adventures with lions and leopards, with crocodiles and hippopotami—crocs and hippos as they are familiarly called. Sometimes a boat is upset by a hippo or a boatman carried off by a croc. Once when Dr. Laws and Dr. Elmslie were camping in the open, they were wakened through the night by a lion tearing their tent down. And a lady missionary of our acquaintance can tell of a leopard which took possession of her verandah one night, attacked her bedroom door with its claws, and finally leapt on to the roof of the cottage and began to tear off the thatch, which was its only covering.

But in those early days there were other and special dangers. Around the settlers there were fierce savages who often showed themselves unfriendly, while Arab slave-hunters hated them with a heartiness due not only to the invariable antipathy of the Crescent to the Cross, but to a premonition that the coming of this little band of Christian men presaged the downfall of their profitable traffic. Above all fever raged continually at Cape Maclear, and death was busy. "A queer country this," a visitor to Africa once said to Dr. Laws, "where the only things of interest you have to show me are the graves." "Yes," replied the doctor, "but they are the milestones of Christianity to the regions beyond." Milestones of this kind were frequent at first, and by and by it became evident that Cape Maclear was little better than a "white man's grave." In order, therefore, to secure a healthier site, as well as one which would be more central for the command of the whole lake, the headquarters of the settlement were transferred to Bandawé, nearly midway up the western shore.

The wisdom of this change was soon abundantly proved. Bandawé was not only much healthier, but lay in the heart of a populous district, with ready access to several large and influential tribes. The work of the Mission began to extend with wonderful rapidity along the lake coast and far into the interior. But success itself brought fresh dangers and trials.

One of the greatest difficulties lay in the perpetual onslaughts made upon the more peaceful people of the lake shore by the fierce Angoni warriors of the west. These Angoni were descended from a branch of the great Zulu family, and were possessed of all the characteristics of that brave but cruel race. Their fathers had crossed the Zambesi from the south, and carried death and terror all over Nyasaland and right on to Tanganyika. Their chief settlements were on the uplands to the west of Bandawé, and none suffered more from their periodical and merciless raids than the tribes in the neighbourhood of the Mission. For fear of the Angoni these poor people, who lived largely by fishing, were compelled to huddle themselves by the thousand within stockades, or to build their houses on piles in deep water (recalling the "crannogs" of our Celtic ancestors), or on rocky islets scattered about over the surface of the lake. When the white men came to Bandawé great numbers of the natives settled in the immediate vicinity, hoping to be safe under their protection. A great protection the missionaries undoubtedly were, and yet the history of Livingstonia in those days was constantly overcast by the shadow of brutal and pitiless massacre. Every now and then a band of the Angoni would make a rush by night upon a defenceless village, stabbing the inhabitants with their cruel, broad-bladed spears; and in the morning, when word came to Dr. Laws and he set out to do all that could be done by medical skill and Christian pity, he would find scores of unfortunate victims lying on the ground weltering in their own blood. "The Bandawé Mission journal," says Mr. Jack, the historian of Livingstonia, "reads in some places like the history of a bloody campaign, owing to the frequent attacks of these mountain warriors."

Expostulations with these people in their heathen state was useless, for murder for its own sake was part of their very life and creed. It soon became evident that the only way of turning them from their paths of blood was to turn them into Christians. A young converted Kaffir called William Koyi, who knew the Zulu language, was settled amongst them in the first place, and did his best to teach them a higher way of life. He was of course in constant peril, and day by day there went on all around him things which were enough to break even an African's heart, and which by and by sent him prematurely to his grave. "A woman carrying a pot of beer would be killed in broad daylight in order to get the beer and prevent detection. A scream would be heard in the evening, and on inquiring the cause he would be told that it was a worn-out slave who had been put out for the hyenas to devour, as being no longer able to take care of himself. Skeletons of persons murdered were to be seen lying about many villages and in the bush."

Still Koyi's life and words were not without their impression, and when Dr. Laws secured from Scotland in Dr. Elmslie a medical missionary for the Angoni themselves, a striking work of reformation began among these savages. Not all at once, however, for there were sections of the tribe which were unwilling to give up their former practices, and several years after Dr. Elmslie's arrival there took place in a village beside the lake one of the worst raids in the whole experience of the Mission. A band of Angoni crept down through the night upon the hapless people. At the door of every hut a full-armed warrior took his stand and ordered the inmates to come out. As they appeared, the men and boys were immediately dispatched with spears, while the girls and women were seized and bound with bark ropes. In the morning no male was left in the place, and more than 300 captive women sat trembling on the ground, the Angoni meantime feasting themselves on the food and beer of their victims.

But even here this tale of bloodshed does not end. During the night a fugitive had succeeded in carrying word of these events to a station about twelve miles off, where there were two white men, agents of the African Lakes Company. These brave fellows resolved to make an attempt to rescue the women. Seizing their guns and gathering a force of about 100 natives, they made a rapid march upon the village. But no sooner did the Angoni see them advancing than they determined to slaughter their captives wholesale rather than allow them to escape. And so before the very eyes of the rescue-party there began a horrible scene—women screaming for mercy, women wrestling for dear life with armed savages, women and girls writhing in their death agonies on the ground. A sharp fight followed between the Angoni and the traders, but after the former were driven off, a missionary in the locality who had hurried to the spot found that while about 200 of the women and girls had been saved, 132 of them were speared to death, and all around the bush was full of dead and wounded men and boys.

It is one of the triumphs of the Livingstonia Mission that this whole Angoni people, who once lived solely for war, are now peaceful subjects of King Edward. On September 2nd, 1904, they placed themselves by their own free act under the administration of the British Government. Sir Alfred Sharpe, H.M. Commissioner for British Central Africa, accompanied by Lady Sharpe as well as by several of the Livingstonia missionaries, met the Angoni nation in a great *indaba*, and arranged to their complete satisfaction the terms on which Angoniland was taken over by Great Britain. One of the conditions was that the police force should be entirely drawn from the Angoni themselves; another that Yakobé, a nephew of one of their own chiefs and a man who received his education at the Livingstonia Institution, should be appointed the head of this native police. The change wrought by years of Christian teaching is significantly shown by the fact that throughout the whole *indaba* the Commissioner was unattended by a single armed soldier, and that, armed himself with nothing but paper and pencil, and with his wife by his side, he sat all day in the midst of thousands of Angoni warriors in all their panoply of shields and spears.

The following month there appeared in the *Aurora*, a journal which is published in Livingstonia in the English language, and is entirely set up and printed by natives, a graphic account of the day's proceedings from the pen of one of the missionaries who was present. With much justice he remarks that the scene inevitably suggested other and very different chapters in the history of the expansion of the British Empire. "Peace hath her victories no less renown'd than war," and in this case the teaching and influence of a little band of Christian men and women have gained a province for the British Crown without the firing of a single shot or the shedding of a drop of human blood.

But even more distressing at one time than the raids of the Angoni were the ravages of the Arab slave-traders throughout Nyasaland. And hereby hangs another chapter in the romantic tale of Livingstonia. Over the Angoni the white men always had some influence, but over the Arabs they had none. It was contrary to their principles to take up arms against them, and so they had to look on while outrage and murder were perpetrated, all that they could do being to make their stations sanctuaries where at least the escaped captive would be safe and free. Even this right, however, was challenged by the Arabs, who by and by in certain districts of the country declared open war upon the white men, including along with the missionaries the agents of the African Lakes Company, which, as will presently be explained, stood, and still stands, to the Mission in a very close relation of sympathy and co-operation. Out of a multitude of episodes in this Arab war one may be selected which in its thrilling character, as Mr. Jack very fitly says, recalls the defence of the Residency at Lucknow during the heroic days of the Indian Mutiny.

Mlozi, one of the greatest of the Arab traders, proclaimed himself Sultan of a large district near the head of the lake, and intimated to the whole Kondé tribe that they must consider themselves his slaves. To escape from his tyranny many of the people flocked to Karonga, where the African Lakes Company had a station under the charge of Mr. L. M. Fotheringham; whereupon Mlozi besieged the station with a force of five hundred men armed with rifles. Fortifying his post as well as he could, Mr. Fotheringham sent word to Mr. Bain, the nearest missionary, asking for his help. By a forced march of twenty hours Mr. Bain succeeded in reaching Karonga and making his way into the station. Shortly after there arrived most opportunely from the other side of the lake four additional white men, including Dr. Tomory, of the London Missionary Society, and Mr. Alfred (now Sir Alfred) Sharpe, who has since risen to the distinguished position of H.M. Commissioner for British Central Africa. For five days and nights the Arabs poured in an incessant fire upon this little band of six Europeans assisted by about fifty armed natives. The defence was conducted with much skill and courage. Deep pits were dug in the sands for the women and children, while behind barriers of boxes and bales the fighting men kept the Arabs at bay. The escape of the partv with their lives was almost miraculous, for often on waking from a brief nap snatched in the trenches, they would find their pockets full of sand kicked up by the bullets which had been sputtering all around them while they slept. It would have gone hard with them, however, if one of their number had not managed to make his way through the ring of besiegers, and to secure the help of a neighbouring and friendly tribe. He got back just in the nick of time with five thousand of the Wamwanga behind him, and thus reinforced the defenders soon drove off the Arabs in confusion. For two years this state of war continued in Nyasaland, till at length the British Government felt itself obliged to interfere in the interests of humanity as well as of its own subjects. In 1892 a Protectorate was proclaimed, and on the hoisting of the British flag the slave-hunters speedily disappeared, and the people of Nyasaland had rest.

Reference has been made more than once to the African Lakes Company, and its relation to the Livingstonia Mission should now be explained. From the very first, Dr. Laws and his fellow-workers had done what they could to promote industry and commerce among the natives. It was a step forward when the Doctor introduced money into the country, and taught the people the immense advantage of a currency. At first they were rather slow to appreciate the benefit, but before long they became so fully alive to the superiority of coin over calico as a medium of exchange that some of the more cunning ones would hand in a button and say with an air of innocence, "Will you please exchange my money?"

But however convinced the missionaries might be of the truth of Dr. Livingstone's saying, that to teach the Africans to cultivate for our markets was, next to the

Inside a Masai Kraal

Masai Woman Erecting a Kraal

Shows the outside of the kraal

Gospel, the most effectual means of their elevation, it was of course impossible for them to become traders; they had other and more important work to do. Accordingly some of the same philanthropic Christian men in Scotland who had been most active in founding the Livingstonia Mission now conceived the idea of forming a company which, while established on sound business lines, should have as one of its principal objects the promotion of the cause of Christian civilization in East Central Africa. The leader in this enterprise was Mr. James Stevenson, of Glasgow, who will always be remembered in the region of the great lakes by his special and splendid gift of the road which is called after him the Stevenson Road. It is a ten-foot road, involving some difficult feats of engineering, which runs all the way from the north end of Lake Nyasa to the south end of Lake Tanganyika, a distance of more than two hundred miles.

It is scarcely possible to estimate the blessings both positive and negative which the African Lakes Corporation, as it is now called, has conferred upon the whole of the vast region which lies between Lake Tanganyika and the mouths of the Zambesi. It has revolutionized the means of transit by its steamers on the rivers and lakes and by its opening of roads, it has awakened and stimulated the spirit of industry in the natives, and has both created new and higher tastes and made plentiful provision for the growing demands. Negatively it has been a blessing by rigidly keeping out gunpowder and strong drink, and by destroying any hankering on the part of the chiefs after the old traffic in slaves, through its readiness to pay better prices than the Arabs ever gave and also to supply European goods more cheaply. The chiefs know now that it is "highly unprofitable to sell a man, when they can get quite as much for a canoe load of potatoes."

The operations of the Livingstonia Mission now cover an area of thousands of square miles—along the Lake shore, up the Stevenson Road, and far out to the west. Of its various stations and agencies—evangelistic, medical, educational, and industrial—it is impossible to speak in detail. But the heart and soul of all is the "Institution," now called the Overtoun Institution, in honour of Lord Overtoun, to whose munificent generosity it has all along been deeply indebted. Standing on a lofty and healthy plateau, a few hours' climb above the lake and about a hundred miles north of Bandawé, it is a veritable hive of varied industry. Into its schools pupils are gathered from all parts of the country and from different tribes speaking quite distinct languages. Here young men are trained as evangelists or as dispensary and hospital assistants, while others are taught bookkeeping and fitted to become clerks in the service of the Government or of the Lakes Company. Carpentry, bricklaying, engineering, printing, and other useful trades are imparted by skilled artisans from Scotland. Here, too, under a scientific agriculturist, there is carried on a work of gardening, farming, and arboriculture, for which the British Government has made a free grant to the Mission of one hundred square miles of land. The beautiful Manchewé Falls have been bridled, so as to supply the plateau with electric light as well as with motor power to drive machinery. A splendid zigzag road has been cut from the lake right up the precipitous shoulders of Mount Waller, on the summit of which the Institution stands. The Institution is provided with the telegraph and telephone, it rejoices in a literary and debating society, a periodical of its own, and many another fruit of civilization. All this besides the work which day by day lies nearest to its heart—the work of Christian evangelization, by means of which so many thousands of persons young and old have been brought into the faith and fellowship of the Christian Church.

In the General Assembly of the Free Church of Scotland in 1874, before Livingstonia had begun to be, the late Dr. Stewart of Lovedale made a speech proposing that such a Mission should be founded, in which he drew a picture of a beautiful dream-city of the future that had risen up before his mind. It is not too much to say that the foundation stones of this city of dream and hope have already been laid :—

"What I would now humbly suggest as the truest memorial of Livingstone is—the establishment by this Church, or several Churches together, of an institution at once industrial and educational, to teach the truths of the Gospel and the arts of civilized life to the natives of the country ; and which shall be placed on a carefully selected and commanding spot in Central Africa, where, from its position and capabilities, it might grow into a town, and afterwards into a city, and become a great centre of commerce, civilization, and Christianity. And this I would call LIVINGSTONIA."

For the most part the narrative is based upon Mr. Jack's *Daybreak in Livingstonia* (Oliphant, Anderson, and Ferrier), with an Introduction by Dr. Laws, in which the history of the Livingstonia Mission is carried up to 1900. Use has also been made of Dr. Livingstone's *Narrative of an Expedition to the Zambesi and its Tributaries*, Dr. Elmslie's *Among the Wild Ngoni*, and the pages of the *Aurora*.

CHAPTER X

VORTREKKERS IN BAROTSELAND

The three horsemen at the Great Kei River—François Coillard—Trekking northwards—In the clutches of Lobengula—In Khama's country—The Makari-kari Desert—The Upper Zambesi—King Lewanika of Barotseland—A canoe voyage—Adventure with the Balubale—The coming of the Iron Horse.

ON an autumn day in the year 1875 three horsemen rode out of King William's Town in the Cape Colony, and turned their faces to the north for the long journey to Basutoland, a distance of 300 miles, which lay before them. As they rode on side by side they talked earnestly about a movement, in which they were all deeply interested, for extending the influence of the French Protestant Mission in Basutoland into the vast region to the north between the Limpopo and Zambesi rivers—virgin soil in those days so far as Christian teaching was concerned. Of the three one was a soldier, Major Malan by name. He was a Swiss by birth, who had become an officer in the British Army, but had resigned his commission in order to devote himself to Christian work among the native races of Africa. The other two, M. Coillard and M. Mabille, were Frenchmen, agents of the celebrated Basutoland Mission carried on by Protestants from France. These two had already done their part in building up a strong native Church among the valleys of that

"Switzerland of South Africa," and now they were lifting up their eyes to wider horizons and thinking of the needs of the tribes to the far north.

When the trio reached the Great Kei River they plunged in and made the crossing. As they landed on the northern bank a common impulse seized them, and springing from their horses they knelt down under the shadow of a bush and devoted themselves before God to the new enterprise on which they had set their hearts. Then when they had remounted, Major Malan, as if he had been leading a cavalry charge, waved his hat, spurred his horse, and galloped up the hill with his two friends fast at his heels, shouting in his enthusiasm, "Three soldiers ready to conquer Africa." These men meant what they said. That incident marked the origin of the Barotse Mission. And it is of one of the three, M. Coillard, and how he fulfilled the vow he took beneath that bush by the Kei River, that this chapter is to tell.

When the honour of leading an expedition to the north of the Limpopo was entrusted to M. Coillard by the Church of Basutoland, he was no tyro in the work of the pioneer. In fact he had been pioneering already for twenty years. For most of that time he and his wife, a brave Scotchwoman, had been content to live in a waggon, after the fashion of the South African "vortrekker," or at best in a poor hut. He had lately built himself a comfortable house and planted a garden round it; but of the fruit of that garden Madame Coillard and he were never to eat. The rest of their lives was to be spent in seeking to do for the tribes of the Zambesi what they had already done for the Basuto people.

IN THE CLUTCHES OF LOBENGULA

Starting from Basutoland with four native catechists as well as with his wife and niece, a girl of eighteen, M. Coillard trekked with his ox caravan right through the territories of the Transvaal Republic, crossed the Limpopo, and plunged into a trackless wilderness where, like sailors on the ocean, they had nothing to guide them but their compass and the stars. Their first rude experience was at the hands of Masonda, a cowardly and treacherous Mashona chief. He received them with great protestations of friendship, but the very next day tried to decoy them to the edge of a frightful precipice, with the view of hurling them down. Being frustrated in his murderous plan, he sought some compensation in robbing them of seventeen of their oxen before he would allow them to leave his country.

They had not long escaped from the clutches of this rascal when they fell into the hands of a savage still more dangerous because much more powerful—the redoubtable Lobengula, king of the Matabele. A band of Lobengula's men seized them and dragged them off to Bulawayo, at that time the capital of the Matabele, on the charge of having entered the king's territory without his permission. For three weeks they were hurried by forced marches across a very rough country, while every comfort was denied them. Even to wash in a wayside stream was a crime, respect for this black monarch requiring them to appear in his presence with all the dirt and sweat of the three weeks upon them as a proof that they had obeyed his summons with the utmost alacrity. When they came in sight of Bulawayo they were met by a witch doctor, who performed a ceremony of exorcism. Dipping a gnu's tail in a slimy green mixture, he applied this spiritual disinfectant liberally to every member of the company, back and front. For M. Coillard, as a rival sorcerer, he reserved a double dose of his medicine, dashing the liquid into his face and all over his clothes.

For nearly four months Lobengula kept the Coillards prisoners, but finally he contented himself with expelling them from his country, and forbidding them ever to return to Matabeleland. There seemed no alternative now but to retreat, and so with heavy hearts the little caravan made their way for hundreds of miles to the south-west till they reached Khama's country, where that well-known Christian chief, then quite a young man, received them with the utmost kindness. He warmly approved of their purpose to push northwards, and did all in his power to further their plans. And as a good deal of communication went on between his own country and that of Lewanika, king of the Barotse on the Upper Zambesi, he sent a body of envoys along with M. Coillard all the way to Barotseland, to urge upon Lewanika the advisability of welcoming the white teachers. It was largely through Khama's influence that the way was thus finally opened up for an advance to the very threshold of Central Africa.

Having returned to the south and also made a voyage to Europe for the furtherance of his new plans, M. Coillard was at length in a position to trek to the north again. This time he was accompanied not only by Basuto helpers, but by a young Swiss clergyman, M. Jeanmairet, and by two white artisans, one English and the other Scotch, whose services proved absolutely invaluable to the enterprise. In the interval Barotseland had been visited by Mr. F. S. Arnot, of whom something will be said in another chapter. He had spent a considerable time in Lewanika's capital, facing endless privations and trials, but had at length been compelled by illness to leave the unhealthy Zambesi basin and start on that long march to Benguela which led him eventually to the Garenganze country. It was to take up and carry on the work which Arnot had tried to begin that M. Coillard now turned his face towards the Upper Zambesi.

Having once more reached Khama's country, the caravan next crossed the Makari-kari Desert, with its swamps and sands, its almost impenetrable jungles of thorn, its dreary death-like solitudes. Here dwell the Bushmen, the Masaroa, as they are called by the tribes of the Zambesi basin. These people would have proved troublesome but for the fact that Khama, whose strong arm was respected over all that region, had once more sent a party of his men to accompany the travellers all the way to their destination. After the desert came vast virgin forests. Through these the cumbrous waggons with their long teams of oxen, so suitable for movement on the open veldt, could only be forced with heart-breaking toil and to the destruction of nearly everything that was breakable. Constant zigzags were indispensable, but in spite of all care in trying to get round the trees an unexpected branch would every now and then make a clean sweep of a waggon, so that portmanteaus, trunks, tool-boxes, books, and haberdashery lay in wild confusion on the ground.

At length to their intense delight they came in sight of the great river just where the Upper Zambesi joins its waters with those of the Chobe. But their difficulties were far from over. The cruelties of Lewanika had brought about a revolution in Barotseland; the king had been driven into exile, and the whole country was in a state of anarchy. It was impossible in the meantime to proceed up the river to the capital, and for months the expedition could do little but wait on the turn of events. At length there came a counter-revolution. Lewanika was restored to the throne, and signalized his triumph by a massacre of the rebel chiefs, their children also being put to death without exception, while their wives were divided among the conquerors. After all this had taken place, Lewanika gave permission to M. Coillard to advance into the heart of Barotseland and to begin work not far from Lealuyi, as the capital was called.

Seldom has pioneer work been carried on in the face of more crushing difficulties and bitter disappointments than those which were encountered for several years by this heroic Frenchman and his colleagues. It soon turned out that Lewanika cared nothing for the introduction of Christianity among his people; all that he wanted was to reap material advantages from the presence of the white men in his country. Whatever was theirs he considered to be his, and when he found them less pliable than his own cringing subjects, he treated them to threats and studied insults, or tried to starve them out by a system of boycott in which all the markets were closed against them. Meanwhile they had to witness day by day the worst horrors of African barbarism—the inhumanities of the slave trade, the fruits of a universal belief in witchcraft, the open practice of murder. Slave children were offered to the Coillards whom they could not buy, and yet they knew that to refuse might be to sign the death-warrant of a child. It was impossible to walk a few steps from their door without striking their feet against a skull or a collection of half-charred human bones, marking the spot where men and women had been burned alive. Whoever gave the slightest offence to Lewanika was at once ordered off to execution. But most painful of all were the witchcraft ordeals which constantly went on. If misfortune came to any one he had only to accuse a neighbour of having used sorcery against him, and the accused must submit to trial by ordeal. The method in Barotseland was by boiling water. A pot of water was set on a large fire. As soon as the water boiled, the poor wretch had to plunge his hands into it, and if the skin peeled off, as of course it almost invariably did, he was at once dragged away to a cruel death. From this fate no one was safe, man or woman, young or old, chief or slave.

But the power of truth, backed by such patience and heroism as were shown by the Coillards, gradually began to tell. Lewanika grew ashamed of his cruelties, and came to have a larger sense of his responsibilities as the master of a vast territory stretching from the Kalahari Desert on the south to the watershed between the Congo and the Zambesi systems on the north. He was naturally a most intelligent man, possessed of a mechanical skill exceedingly rare in an African prince. He had a workshop of his own in which he spent his leisure hours, and could turn out almost anything he wanted, from a canoe to a harmonica or a delicately carved ivory bracelet. Canoe-building was a speciality of the Barotse, for like all the Zambesians they are essentially a river people. But the state-barge of the king's own designing, sixty feet long and manned by fifty rowers, was a structure of which the whole nation was proud. Though his heart was difficult to reach, his intelligence and ambition could be appealed to, and by and by he grew eager to see education, industry, and civilization develop among his people. As the representatives of all these good things he came to trust M. Coillard and his colleagues, and to favour the progress of Christianity among his subjects.

When he had at length secured a firm footing in the capital, Coillard began to think of the various tribes on the higher reaches of the Zambesi, which were more or less under Lewanika's sway, and one of the most interesting chapters of his striking book, *On the Threshold of Central Africa*, is that which tells of a voyage of exploration far up towards the sources of the river. He was accompanied by forty men in a flotilla of ten canoes, and, in order that canoeing might be easy, the expedition was made at a time shortly after the height of the annual floods, when the Zambesi Valley was all under water. The plain at this season "is a floating prairie, enamelled with flowers; rosetted water-lilies, with their delicate tints of blue, pink, and white; and a kind of convolvulus which proudly erects her great magenta trumpets, only dipping them reluctantly as our canoes go by. But it is also diversified by tall grass and reeds, through which we have to force our way."

Far up the river they met a venerable man, nearly blind, who had seen Livingstone, and who pointed out a spot where the great traveller had camped and which was still known by his name. When Coillard spoke of Jesus he listened attentively and said, "It is just what Nyaka (i.e. 'The Doctor') used to say." In one place where the Mission party held a meeting with the people and sang a hymn, they were astonished to find that all present could join in it heartily. "Who taught it to you?" they asked; and the people shouted, "Bangueta." Then M. Coillard saw how the seed he had been sowing had silently spread like "bread cast upon the waters," for Bangueta had been a pupil in his own school at Lealuyi.

At length they reached a district so far up the river that Lewanika's name was no longer the protection it had hitherto been. They were now in the country of the Balubale, whose chief was called Kakenge. A mob of young men armed with guns met them, who demanded to know what the white man meant by coming into Kakenge's country with a band of Barotse, and without having obtained his permission. They also sought to exact the homage or tax which Kakenge imposed upon all traders coming to that land. Coillard told them that he was not a merchant or even a traveller, but a *Moruti*, i.e. a teacher, and that he had come among them to teach the things of God. They took him into the presence of the king, who was throned on a stool, clothed in a coloured blanket, and shaded by an enormous blue cotton umbrella held by a slave. All Coillard's explanations were treated by Kakenge as lies, and after breaking into a passionate speech, he suddenly turned his back on the missionary and disappeared into his harem.

Things were looking bad, especially as the expedition had been refused all food since coming to Kakenge's country, and by this time they were nearly starving. But the situation grew still more serious when two of M. Coillard's men, who had contracted blood-brotherhood with some of the Balubale, obtained secret information that out of pure hatred for the Barotse Kakenge had sworn to destroy the whole party, and had already given orders for their massacre.

That night not one of the company slept. All of them, heathen and Christian alike, were praying to God. And next day a wonderful change had come over Kakenge's mind, for he sent them a plentiful supply of millet and fowls and sweet potatoes, and when they went in a body to the court to thank him for his kindness, told them that he had come to believe in their good intentions, and asked them to forget his ill-temper of the past days.

This was the farthest point reached by M. Coillard in his advance from the south towards the heart of Africa; and at this point our account of the labours and wanderings of this brave and devoted Frenchman must stop. Those who wish to know more about him and his work will find the story fully told in his own book.

There have been wonderful changes on the Upper Zambesi in recent years. The Barotse kingdom now forms a part of that vast stretch of British African territory which is known as Rhodesia. King Lewanika himself has paid a visit to England and been presented at King Edward's Court. A mighty bridge now spans the Victoria Falls. Through the regions where Coillard once toiled slowly with his labouring teams the Cape to

Cairo railway now carries its passengers in swift and luxurious ease. But nothing can dim the honour of the heroic Christian "Vortrekker" who left his home in the fair Basuto valleys more than a generation ago, and turned the poles of his ox-waggons towards the land beyond the Limpopo.

The material for the above chapter is drawn from M. Coillard's *On the Threshold of Central Africa* (Hodder and Stoughton).

CHAPTER XI

A PIONEER IN GARENGANZE

King Msidi's letter—Garenganze—Fred S. Arnot—His earlier travels—The expedition from Benguela—An African camp—The bees-wax hunters—Watershed of the continent—Reception by Msidi—A night with cheetahs and hyenas—Horrors of the slave traffic—The saviours of Africa.

SOME twenty years ago a young Scotchman, Fred S. Arnot by name, who was travelling from the Upper Zambesi towards Benguela on the West African coast, met a company of men from the far interior with a letter in their charge. The letter was sent by Msidi, king of Garenganze, and contained an earnest appeal that white men would come to his country. Arnot did not doubt that by white men Msidi meant traders, by whom he and his people might be enriched. He was no trader, but a pioneer missionary who had already crossed Africa from east to west seeking to do good to the native tribes, and who at that very time was wondering where it would be best for him to settle down more permanently as a Christian teacher. Yet Msidi's appeal came to him with all the force of a personal call, and he decided that, as soon as he reached Benguela, he would make preparations for a march to the Garenganze country.

Garenganze lies to the west of Lakes Moero and

Bangweolo, near the latter of which Dr. Livingstone died. It is thus in the very heart of Central Africa, some 1500 miles each way from the Indian Ocean and the Atlantic. It has now been absorbed by the Congo Free State, but at that time it was a powerful independent kingdom. The people, judged by an African standard, had attained to some measure of civilization; and King Msidi, in the same comparative sense, was an able and enlightened monarch. The country was one of the most densely populated in that part of the continent, famed far and near for the abundance of its corn, rice, sugar-cane, and other agricultural products; and not less for its copper mines, which were worked by the inhabitants, who cleansed and smelted the copper out of the ore with remarkable skill. Up to 1886, the year of Arnot's arrival, only two Europeans had visited Msidi's dominions—a German traveller from the east and a Portuguese from the south; and in both cases the visits were very brief. Livingstone had never reached Garenganze, though he was drawing near it when he died at Ilala, not far from the shores of Lake Bangweolo.

But though Livingstone himself never entered Garenganze, it was a pioneer of Livingstone's own type who first brought the Christian Gospel to Msidi's people. Fred S. Arnot may be described as one of the most remarkable of the many heroes of African travel, not so much for what he actually accomplished as for the manner and spirit in which he accomplished it. It is here that he especially reminds us of Dr. Livingstone. His methods of progress were not those of the well-equipped and hustling explorer, but of the lonely wanderer who makes his way, quietly, patiently, and in the spirit of love, from village to village and from tribe to tribe. He had already served his apprenticeship to African travel. Landing in Natal in 1881, he had slowly trekked through the Orange Free State and the Transvaal to Khama's country, had next crossed the awful Kalahari Desert, and so made his way to the Zambesi. A whole year was occupied in this journey, which brought with it many experiences of danger and suffering. Repeatedly he had been on the point of perishing from hunger or thirst. Once, after marching in the desert for three days and nights without a drop of water, he met some Bushmen, who supplied him with a drink after their own fashion. They dug a pit in the sand, and sank long tubes made of reeds into the ground at the bottom. By and by water began to gather, as they knew it would, at the sunk end of the tube. They invited Arnot to drink. He tried, but was quite unable to suck the water up the long tube. The Bushmen, whom frequent practice had made adepts in the art, accordingly sucked it up for him, and then spat it out into a tortoise shell and handed it to the stranger. "It was frothy stuff," he writes, "as you may imagine; but I enjoyed it more than any draught I ever took of Loch Katrine water."

His ways of getting food had sometimes been peculiar also. On the Zambesi he often depended for his supper on the crocodiles, which are very plentiful in that great river. Not that he ate those loathsome reptiles, but he was thankful at least to share their meals. When one of the larger game comes down to the river to drink, the crocodile creeps up stealthily, seizes the animal by the nose, drags it under water, and then hides the body under the river bank until it becomes almost putrid. When it is "high" enough to suit his taste, Master Croc brings it to the surface and enjoys a feast. The hungry traveller used to lie on the bank and watch one of those animals as it rose, with perhaps a quarter of an antelope in its jaws. Then he fired at its head and compelled it to drop its supper, and in this way provided himself with his own. He admits that it was anything but a dainty repast.

Coming at last to the malarious Barotse Valley on the Upper Zambesi, he settled down there for two years, doing what he could to teach the people and to wean them from their habitual cruelties. But at last his health completely broke down, and he decided to march for the west coast in the company of Senhor Porto, a Portuguese traveller who was going in that direction. It shows the stuff of which Arnot was made that, in spite of his reduced condition, he decided to ride on an ox, instead of being carried like his fellow-traveller in a *machila* or hammock. The reason he gave was that "that would be too comfortable a way of travelling, and might make me discontented and extravagant at other times." It was on this journey from the Barotse Valley to Benguela that he fell in with the messengers of King Msidi, as mentioned above, and resolved to make Garenganze the goal of another expedition in the interior.

It was in the beginning of June, 1885, that he set out on this journey, which was to occupy between eight and nine months. In its earlier stages the march lay along a well-trodden route in Portuguese territory, from Benguela to Bihé. First came the low-lying desert region between Benguela and Cantumbela, which is just at the foot of

In the Footsteps of the Slave Trader

the hills that mark the beginning of the lower section of the characteristic African plateau. These hills climbed, he found himself for a time in a fertile tropical country; but by and by another and a higher table-land rose before him, on climbing which he passed so suddenly out of the climate of the tropics that he could almost mark the line of demarcation between trees like the baobab and the more familiar vegetation of the temperate zone.

At Bihé Arnot had no end of difficulty in getting porters to accompany him on his tramp into the unknown regions which now stretched before him like an unexplored ocean. But at length he succeeded in gathering a motley company, some of the members of which he has sketched for us as typical African characters:—

"Chipooka stammers as he speaks, but is lively under all circumstances; has a bad festering toe, which, however, does not prevent him carrying his sixty-pound load. Though limping badly, his only response to expressions of sympathy is a broad grin. Saombo is another representative man, perfectly hideous in his looks, but vanity has made his ugliness appear comical. All who come to the camp, he seems to think, have come to see him. So, as soon as a few strangers gather, he is not prepared for more hut-building or wood-cutting, but must go and sit down in front of them, laughing and clapping his thighs with delight, and trying to crack jokes. Then we have the sulky grumbler amongst us, who has always something to complain of. Now his load is not right, next his rations, then his pay; or a thorn pricks his foot, and he can carrry no longer that day. The work has to be done, but certainly not by him."

AN AFRICAN CAMP

Besides his men and his horned steed, for once more he took an ox as his bearer, Arnot numbered on his camp-roll a faithful dog and a parrot. Senhor Porto, his recent companion, was accustomed to carry a cock with him on his travels by way of an animated chronometer, whose morning crows announced to all that it was time to commence the day's march. Arnot found a cock unnecessary, the cooing of the wood-pigeons being a sufficient signal to his men that dawn had come and that it was time to be stirring. But he recommends a parrot as a valuable addition to the resources of an African caravan. His Poll was of great service in keeping up the spirit of his boys. It was a true Mark Tapley of a bird, seeming as if it watched for opportunities when there would be some credit in being jolly. When every one was dull and depressed it would suddenly make some ridiculous remark or break out in imitation of an old man's laugh. So it relieved the monotony of the march, and put the weary carriers into good humour again.

Mr. Arnot gives us a clear picture of the daily routine of an African journey. By break of day the camp is astir, for the porters are always anxious to get well along the road in the cool of the morning. Breakfast they do not trouble about, being content to have one good meal at the close of the day. They buckle on their belts, shoulder their loads of 60 lb. each, and trot off through the forest. Probably some one begins a solo in a high key, and all join lustily in the chorus. One or two halts are made, and there may be considerable delay when rivers have to be crossed. But for the most part all press on steadily for the next camping-place, which is generally reached by noon.

When a site for the camp has been fixed upon, some of the party are sent out to the nearest villages to buy food—the staple diet being maize meal made into a thick porridge, of which an African will consume an astonishing quantity. Meanwhile the others busy themselves with erecting shelters for the night. Poles are cut down in the forest, and stacked after the manner in which soldiers pile their rifles. Against these, branches are rested, and if it is the rainy season a thatching of the long African grass is added. Then fires are kindled to cook the supper, and these are kept up through the night to scare away wild beasts. An African camp at night, says Mr. Arnot, would make a fine picture on canvas—the blazing fires; the black faces clustered round them; the men singing, talking, laughing; and all about a pitchy darkness, made doubly deep by the dense shadows of bush and forest. Every night it was the leader's habit to sit with his men around the camp fires, trying in every possible way to convey to them intelligent thoughts as to his mission. He felt that it was of the first importance that they should understand something about his message and his motive in bringing it, and so should be able to give an answer to the thousands of natives who would be sure to bombard them with questions as to who this white man was and why he had come.

One of the districts traversed by the caravan was the Chibowke country, a land of beeswax-hunters, who spend weeks on end in the depths of the forest gathering beeswax to sell to the Bihé traders, and living meanwhile on little else than wild honey. A high region was crossed where one day, in the space of two or three hours, they saw the fountain-heads of streams which flow respectively into the Congo and the Zambesi, and so ultimately into the Atlantic on the one side of the continent and the Indian Ocean on the other. Then came a wide tract where population was scanty and food scarce, and Arnot had a good deal of trouble with his men. They demanded more rations, and especially more meat. One day they flung down their loads crying, "Monare" (their name for Arnot), "give us meat. Why don't you hunt? You are starving us." Anxious though he was to press on, he saw that there was nothing for it but to devote the day to hunting. He seized his gun, forgetting that it was loaded, and as he was pulling off the cover, the charge suddenly went off, shattering the point of his left forefinger. There was no one with him who could dress a wound, and he thought it best to get one of the men to cut off the top joint according to his directions. The accident had a subduing effect on the men, who felt as if they were to blame for it; and in spite of hunger they tramped on bravely. Starvation, however, had begun to stare them in the face when Arnot succeeded one day in shooting two wart-hogs, one of which weighed over 200 lb. and had tusks over a foot long. A time of feasting followed. And as the men marched along once more, their leader heard them saying: "Don't you remember what things we said of the white man and his God? What names we called them! But the white man's God has been with us, and has filled our bodies with pig-meat."

The trials of the long journey were now nearly over. A few days more brought them to the Garenganze country, where, after so many days in a desert region, it was a delight to see fields of grain and abundance of food, and still more to be hospitably received on every hand. On reaching the capital Arnot expected to have an early interview with the king. But it was not Msidi's habit to welcome strangers all at once. For some time the white man was placed in a sort of quarantine, while various tests were employed by witch doctors and diviners to see whether his intentions were good or bad, and "whether his heart was as white as his skin." A little piece of bark, for instance, was placed at night in a certain decoction. If next morning the bark appeared quite sound, that showed that the heart of the new-comer was equally so. If, on the other hand, it was in the least decomposed, the inference was that his heart was rotten, and that he must not be trusted. Fortunately, after several days had been spent in experiments of this kind, everything turned out in Arnot's favour, and the king accorded him a public reception.

The reception was both friendly and imposing. Msidi, an elderly man with a white beard, folded his arms around the traveller in the most fatherly manner, and then introduced him to his wives, of whom he had 500, as well as to his numerous brothers, cousins, and other relatives. Arnot found that Livingstone's name was one to charm with. Msidi had heard of the Doctor's approach from the east in 1873 and of his death at Ilala, and was pleased to learn that his visitor was a man of peace and goodwill like Livingstone, and that he hailed from the same country. He begged Arnot to remain in Garenganze and to build himself a house on any site he pleased; and this was the beginning of the Garenganze Mission.

CHEETAHS AND HYENAS

For two years Arnot toiled on all alone in that remote land, making tours of exploration from the capital into the surrounding districts. In most places the people had never seen a white man before, and his appearance created a great sensation. The very print of his boots on the path was a portent. "His feet," they said, "are not a man's feet; they are the feet of a zebra." He had many strange adventures and not a few narrow escapes. But perhaps his most trying experience was when he spent a whole night in the open, alone and in pitch darkness, surrounded by a ring of hungry wild beasts.

He had gone out in the company of a native to shoot antelopes at a time when food was scarce, and after a long tramp had succeeded in getting near to a herd and bringing down three. By this time, however, the sun was setting, and the dismal howl of the hyena began to be heard. The nearest village was far off, but Arnot sent his companion to bring assistance, resolving to keep guard himself over the game throughout the night. He had no means of kindling a fire, and to make matters worse, his ammunition was all expended, so that he had no weapons but an empty rifle and a hunting knife. One of the antelopes, which lay at a distance of about a hundred yards from the rest, he soon had to surrender, but he marched up and down beside the other two, shouting and stamping and making as much noise as possible. The cold grew so intense by and by that he drew his hunting knife and skinned one of the antelopes as best he could in the dark, rolled himself in the warm hide, and lay down on the ground. But no sooner had he done this than he heard stealthy footsteps approaching, so that he had to spring

ARNOT DEFENDING HIS FOOD FROM WILD BEASTS

Food was scarce, so he went out shooting accompanied by a native. He succeeded in bringing down three antelopes, and then he sent the native to get help to carry the game to camp. Meanwhile he had to mount guard. With no fire and no cartridges left, he had to keep cheetahs and hyenas at bay by shouting and stamping his feet right through the night. Fortunately no lions happened to come by.

up again. Only by rushing up and down for several hours, shouting all the time, was he able to keep his savage assailants at bay. When daylight came he saw from the footprints that he had been surrounded through the night by a band of hyenas and cheetahs. It was fortunate for him that no lions had been attracted to the spot.

For two years, as we have said, Arnot held this missionary outpost single-handed before any reinforcements arrived, and during all that time he never had a chance of receiving even a letter from the outer world. The oppression of this loneliness was increased by the heathen vices and cruelties which went on in Garenganze just as in other parts of Darkest Africa. All around him in particular the horrors of the slave-traffic prevailed and infants were constantly done to death because their owners had no use for them. The slave-traders regarded them as positive nuisances, not only encumbering their mothers on the march, but preventing them from carrying loads of ivory or some other commodity. And as no one wanted to buy the helpless little creatures, the slavers quite commonly flung them into a river or dashed out their brains against the trunk of a tree. As we read of the sights that were to be seen in Garenganze day by day, we do not wonder that the saying passed from mouth to mouth among the slave population, "Cheer up, slave! The Emperor (death) is coming along to save you."

One day the body of a fine little boy, with a fatal spear gash through and through, was picked up on the road. It was a child whose owner shortly before had pressed Arnot to take it. Another infant whom he had felt unable to accept was thrown into the bush and devoured by the beasts. And so he was led to resolve that he must at all costs save these poor slave children—a decision which soon brought him an embarrassing family of youngsters to whom he had to take the place of both father and mother.

Not less painful than the accompaniments of slavery was the prevalence of human sacrifice. Msidi never entered upon any enterprise without seeking to ensure himself of success by putting some one to death. No one knew beforehand who the victim might be. The king simply said that So-and-so was to be taken, and straightway the appointed man or woman was led out to the slaughter.

There is a heroism of patient endurance and continuance as well as a heroism of bold achievement. It sometimes needs more courage to hold the trenches than to lead the forlorn charge. Arnot showed himself a hero in both kinds. His marches through Africa, first from Natal to the West Coast, and then again from Benguela to Garenganze, reveal some of the best qualities of the intrepid explorer. But his quiet persistence in his chosen work as a messenger of Christ, through loneliness and sickness, through danger and disappointment, tells of other qualities which are nobler and finer. It is men like this hero of Garenganze who are the true saviours of Africa.

Mr. Arnot's book, from which the above sketch is drawn, is entitled *Garenganze, or Seven Years' Pioneer Mission Work in Central Africa* (London: James E. Hawkins).

CPSIA information can be obtained
at www.ICGtesting.com
Printed in the USA
JSHW040839290322
24358JS00006B/332

9 780880 191036